SERMONS AND LECTURES

OF

E. R. BERNARD

T0371265

SERMONS AND LECTURES

SELECTED FROM

THE REMAINS OF THE LATE

EDWARD RUSSELL BERNARD, M.A.

CANON AND CHANCELLOR OF SALISBURY
AND CHAPLAIN IN ORDINARY
TO H.M. THE KING.

CAMBRIDGE
AT THE UNIVERSITY PRESS
1929

CAMBRIDGE
UNIVERSITY PRESS

University Printing House, Cambridge CB2 8BS, United Kingdom

Cambridge University Press is part of the University of Cambridge.

It furthers the University's mission by disseminating knowledge in the pursuit of
education, learning and research at the highest international levels of excellence.

www.cambridge.org
Information on this title: www.cambridge.org/9781316619988

First published 1929
First paperback edition 2016

A catalogue record for this publication is available from the British Library

ISBN 978-1-316-61998-8 Paperback

CONTENTS

CONTENTS

PREFACE

The following pages are the scanty gleaning of more than fifty years' active and devoted ministry.

From the moment of his ordination in 1867 till his death in 1921, Edward Russell Bernard, so far as fragile health allowed him, never ceased to teach and learn the things pertaining to the Kingdom of God. His early life had been that of a classical scholar. The foundations were soundly laid first at Wimborne Grammar School under Dr William Fletcher from 1852 to 1855, and then at Harrow (1855–1861) under Dr Vaughan, and for one year under Dr Montagu Butler, who once said of him that he was the best Latinist of all his pupils.

His career at Oxford was brilliant. He went up to Exeter with an open scholarship in 1861. He won the "Hertford" in 1863, and the "Craven" in 1866. He obtained a first class in Classical Moderations and a second in *Litt. Hum.*, graduating B.A. in 1866. A Fellowship at Magdalen followed at once, which he retained till 1877. The lighter side of his learning as an undergraduate appears in a note written by himself for Dr E. W. Watson's *Life of John Wordsworth*, recording "a Latin dinner-party, at which Latin only was to be spoken, which Wordsworth and I gave in our joint lodgings in New College Lane on 1st December, 1865. The idea, I think, was his, but the invitations, of course in Latin, were from us both....I do not remember the conversation, but I think we got on pretty well, after a first blank and hopeless endeavour to greet one another as the guests arrived".

Although divinity came to be the main business of his life, he never lost touch with the Classics and if ever the term *humaniste dévot* was deserved, it was so by this Christian scholar.

His Magdalen Fellowship supplied him with the needed title for ordination in the diocese of Norwich, where the Bishop, Dr Pelham, a friend of his father, Thomas Dehany Bernard, found him a sphere of work.

After a year at Blickling near Norwich, where he was curate in sole charge (only seeing his vicar once in all that time, when he was taken to his bedroom to certify that he was still alive), there followed six years in the tiny living of Tarrant Monkton in Dorset. Here he remained till 1876, when his college, Magdalen, presented him to Selborne in the diocese of Winchester. In 1886, his lifelong friend, Dr John Wordsworth, who had just been consecrated Bishop of Salisbury, bestowed upon him the prebendal stall of Combe-cum-Harnham, and three years later called him into residence as one of the four Canons.

In 1894 he was appointed Chancellor of the Cathedral.[1] He resigned the Canonry in 1910, and the Chancellorship in 1917, retaining only the Prebendship. But long after he had shed his active capitular offices, he continued to preach, in his parish church,

[1] His father was simultaneously Chancellor of Wells.

(Wimborne Minster), in other churches in the neighbourhood (very especially in a little mission chapel in an outlying district), and away from home, in the Chapel Royal (he was Honorary Chaplain to Queen Victoria, King Edward and King George, and Chaplain in Ordinary to King George from 1911 till his death), at the Universities, or to public schoolboys; and his message never lost its force.

He was under no illusion as regards the present value or future fate of his sermons. He could not fail to recognise that he had the preacher's gift, and he often lectured on the art of preaching, but "People don't read and won't buy sermons", he would say when he was urged to print his own. And in fact he published but one set, *The Path to Freedom* (five sermons on *Galatians*, Nisbet, 1894), a single sermon in a volume edited by Bishop Barry, and now and then a special discourse in the *Guardian*[1] or in the local press.

Notwithstanding his disclaimer, characteristically modest, I believe that not only will the friends who revered him be glad to have something more to remind them of his piety and wisdom, but that there is, even for those who did not know him, both pleasure and profit to be had from the perusal of his restrained and grave eloquence, where every word is heart-deep, mixt with faith and love and knowledge of the Scriptures, and tried upon a long experience of the world.

"Discreet understanding must go with zeale, and

---

[1] One such, no. ix of the present collection, is reprinted by kind permission of the *Guardian*.

gravity with sincerity; affection is heady without wisedome: this moderates as the other pricks forward: they must be linked inseparably."

So wrote Richard Bernard, Rector of Worksop, in 1607, and no one will say that his namesake did not fulfil the conditions which the old Puritan laid down for a Faithful Shepherd.[1]

In the pulpit Edward Bernard spoke most often on a moral theme, making the Bible shine as a lamp to the feet, and a light upon the Christian path. As for his method, he usually preached from notes—four sides of notepaper, covered with abbreviations and ligatures. Sometimes he wrote a sermon out in full, and it is from what he left of such that the present selection

[1] Cf. *The Faithful Shepherd*, by Richard Bernard, M.A., p. 2.

Richard Bernard (1567–1641), a Christ's man, and a native of Notts or Lincs, was first Rector of Worksop, where he wrote *The Faithful Shepherd*, and from 1615 of Batcombe in Somerset.

He was an interesting figure, in several ways ahead of his times, anticipating John Howard in his pity for prisoners (*Isle of Man*, 1627), and the C.O.S. in his plan for systematic charity (*A Ready Way to Good Works*, 1635). He also espoused the unpopular cause of the unconverted Jews (*Great Mysterie of God's Mercy yet to come*, Part II of *The Seaven golden Candlestickes*, 1621).

Apart from the name there seems to be no connexion between this Richard and our Edward Bernard, whose Huguenot family did not leave France until the Revocation of the Edict of Nantes in 1685. Then Daniel Bernard departed to Jamaica, and engaged in the sugar trade. This brought him into connexion with Bristol, and his great-great-grandson Charles, the father of Thomas Dehany above mentioned, and of Mountague, the great international lawyer, and grandfather of Edward Bernard, settled permanently in England.

has been made. He was not the slave of his manuscript, and although the delivery was not that of an orator, it was impressive and arresting—the point driven home by a pause, a look over his spectacles, an apostrophe, or by a break of the voice under felt emotion, which was most affecting.

He avoided rhetoric and all parade of learning; but he had a high sense of the value of words; and his wide reading (besides his Classics he was a fine Italian scholar, and, what is rarer, at home in the Scandinavian tongues[1]), his general culture, his love of nature, and of his garden, could not but have their effect upon his utterance.

Upon his appointment as Chancellor of Sarum in 1894, the obligation of divinity lectures, which had been in abeyance for 190 years, was revived.[2]

The new Chancellor was exact in the fulfilment of this duty, for which his scholarship and learning and sense of proportion peculiarly fitted him, and during his tenure of the office he gave regularly a course in Lent, and one in Advent, to the great benefit of all concerned. The list of his subjects shows the range of his interests.

[1] Danish was apparently learnt first; then came Icelandic for the sake of the sagas, and then Swedish. He served on the Archbishop of Canterbury's Commission for promoting alliance with the Swedish Church in 1909, and accompanied Dr Wordsworth to Sweden on his visit there in the autumn of that year.

[2] In 1605, when Thomas Hyde was Chancellor (from 1588 till his death in 1618), the Chancellor's divinity lectures were discontinued, and he and his successors were required in lieu of lecturing to preach sermons on Holy Days.

His audience was what you would expect in a cathedral close. Devout ladies and laymen, members of the Chapter, students from the Theological College, city folk, school-mistresses, a few stray clergy. He suited himself to their requirements, and was careful never to speak over their heads, nor to talk down to them.

Three sets of such lectures are here presented. One on the Litany (from the beginning of his Chancellorship), which for accurate information, affectionate loyalty to the Church, and zeal to make the Litany a living instrument of devotion, seems to me unsurpassable of its kind;[1] one delivered a few years later on Hymns, which gave scope for the exercise of his literary taste and gifts; one, a doctrinal course, from the very end of his time, on the Atonement. This last is reprinted by kind permission of the S.P.C.K. from the volume issued at Northumberland House in 1921, now rare if not out of print. The other two are expanded from his manuscript notes.

Of his personal character it is difficult to speak without falling into an exaggeration which would have been repugnant to him; but he was conspicuous in certain fine qualities which must have struck all who came within his range—modesty, sincerity, and generosity. It was not merely a sense of physical

[1] Without being an expert Liturgist he was a close student of the Prayer Book, its history and its use; and he was deeply occupied in Convocation with the Revision of the Prayer Book. One of his few published works is on the Lectionary.

unfitness that led him to decline preferment, e.g. a suffragan bishopric offered him by Dr Davidson of Winchester in 1893, the Deanery of Winchester in 1903, and that of Wells in 1911.

The last-named office must have attracted him strongly; he loved the place with intense affection, and there he was laid to rest under the shadow of the cathedral church of which he might have had the charge. But his favourite motto was ἡσυχάζειν καὶ πράσσειν τὰ ἴδια,[1] and he lived up to it.

He was unshaken in his convictions, but he respected those even of others to whom he was heartily opposed, always giving credit for an honesty equal to his own, and often for a knowledge greater than he possessed, although in this particular he was sometimes mistaken, as is the case with generous and simple-minded men.

His calmness and patience (the latter particularly noticeable when he was teaching) were, I fancy, not inborn, but the result of strict self-discipline, like the courage and care with which he weathered nearly eighty years, many of which were marked by suffering. He strained his heart on the running track at Harrow, which left it permanently irritable. This induced digestive troubles, and combined with a very sensitive nervous temperament to cause the headaches, sleeplessness, and so on, to which he was always subject, especially in earlier life. But although ill-health was

[1] "To be quiet and to do your own business" (I. Thess. iv. 11). He wrote it with his own hand in an album of "Likes and Dislikes", such as was in vogue a generation or two ago.

always in the background, it was not always apparent; at home, and on holiday it was often forgotten by himself and his friends in the keen, nay, youthful enjoyment of things worth enjoying.

During his residence at Salisbury he was very much occupied, and often tired, so that his natural buoyancy was less noticed, and it was no doubt the need of economising his energy that caused his reserve and shyness.

Severe where he suspected pretence or slackness, critical and fastidious in his literary judgments, he was generous to a fault in bestowing praise when he thought it due, for with Cicero he held that *Honos alit artes*.

His practical kindness was lavish; and there must be many who owe their success in life to-day to his help given at a crisis. The shop-assistants and the school-teachers of Salisbury had great cause to bless him. There was his "band" for the former, with regular social meetings in the city and a yearly camp at Wood Green. There was "The Bond" for the latter, a monthly gathering under his presidency at the Church House for the discussion of literature, and for the deeper and more important purpose of drawing together teachers of different grades.

He was particularly attentive to the boys of the choristers' school at Salisbury, feeling as a member of the Chapter, and as Chancellor and *custos puerorum*, an especial obligation to see that the future of children who had served the church well should not be neglected. Besides the Choir School he used to visit the

Training College for Teachers, speaking to the young women on religious or moral subjects; and he used to say that they were the most receptive of all his hearers. He was indeed always deeply interested in education, and he taught regularly and effectively in his own parish schools, both weekday and Sunday. At one time he did a good deal of examining: then he concentrated his energy on higher religious education. He started Societies for the purpose in Winchester and Salisbury, and spent much time and energy on lectures for them. The needs of the clergy greatly occupied his mind. Besides formal work at the Universities in Tripos and Honours schools, conferences of chaplains and heads of theological colleges, he lectured to clergy and ordination candidates, held classes in Hebrew and Greek Testament, and was in close touch with men training for the Ministry for forty years, from 1871 to 1911. One point upon which he especially insisted in speaking to these was the obligation of regular pastoral visiting, which was his own delight when he had a parish, and for which he welcomed every opportunity that presented itself when he ceased to have a cure of souls.

His mind was stored with the beauties of literature, ancient, mediaeval, and modern, and of art and nature; although he never obtruded his knowledge, or imposed his taste in conversation or in sermon, it was felt in both.

His talk was constantly lit up by a delicate humour, and a twinkle of the eye over the foibles of his fellows. He remembered with Bacon, that "God Almighty first planted a garden", and he partook freely of that "purest of human pleasures", bringing to it science and technical skill. He loved the country, and country life, and country folk, in whom he found a kindred simplicity. To sum up, his friendship was a privilege, and his memory is a delight.

H. F. STEWART

July 17, 1929

Edward Russell Bernard, son of the Rev. Thomas Dehany Bernard (Chancellor and Canon of Wells) and of Caroline, daughter of Benjamin Linthorne of High Hall, Dorset.

June 12, 1842. Born in London.
1852–1855. At Wimborne Grammar School under Dr W. Fletcher.
1855–1861. At Harrow under Dr Vaughan and Dr Butler. (Peel and Gregory Medals 1861.)
1861. Scholar of Exeter College, Oxford.
1863. Hertford Scholar.
1866. Craven Scholar.
1866. B.A. (2nd Class *Litt. Hum.*).
1866. Fellow of Magdalen College, Oxford.
1867. Ordained Deacon by Dr Pelham, Bishop of Norwich (on the title of his fellowship).
1867–1869. Curate-in-charge of Blickling, Norfolk.
1868. Classical Moderator; M.A.
1869. Ordained Priest at Norwich.
1870–1876. Vicar of Tarrant Monkton.
1871. Examining Chaplain to Dr Moberly, Bishop of Salisbury.
1876–1889. Vicar of Selborne.
1878. Marriage with Miss Ellen Nicholson of Basing Park.
1881–1883. Examiner in Theological School, Oxford.
1886–1921. Prebendary of Combe-cum-Harnham.
1887–1888. Examiner in Theological Tripos, Cambridge.
1887–1889. Rural Dean of Alton.
1889–1910. Residentiary Canon of Salisbury. In 1910 he left the Close and took up permanent residence at High Hall.
1894–1917. Chancellor of Salisbury Cathedral.
1896–1921. Honorary Chaplain to Queen Victoria, King Edward VII, King George V, Chaplain in Ordinary to King George, 1911.
1905–1907. Rural Dean of Wimborne.
1910–1919. Proctor in Convocation.
April 22, 1921. Died at High Hall.

SUBJECTS OF CHANCELLOR'S LECTURES
FROM 1894 TO 1917

The Character of Jacob (1894). Happiness (1895). The Litany (1896). The Communion Service (1897, 1898). St Paul's Three Journeys (1897). St John on Sin (1898). Parables of the Last Things (1899). Hymns and Hymnology (1899). Minor changes in the R.V. (1899). Doctrine of Sin in the N.T. (1900). The Sabbath (1901). *Proverbs* (1901). Truthfulness (1902). The *Apocrypha* (1902). *Ecclesiasticus* (1903, 1905). Great Moral Teachers (1903). Scripture Penitents (1904). Roman Stoicism (1904). Theology of the N.T. (1905). The Divinity of Our Lord (1906). Christian Ethics (1906). *Pilgrim's Progress* (1907). Justin Martyr (1907). Selfishness (1908). The *Epistle to the Galatians* (1908). Pascal (1909). St Augustine's *Confessions* (1909). The *Book of Wisdom* (1910). The *Purgatorio* (1910). The *Quicunque Vult* (1911). Miracles (1911). The *Paradiso* (1912). The *Epistle to the Ephesians* (1912). Thomas à Kempis (1913). *I. John* xii (1914). The Fall of Jerusalem (1914). Prayer Book Revision (1915). The *Epistle to the Colossians* (1916). The Atonement (1916). *Job* (1917).

PUBLISHED WORKS

Selected Letters of Cicero. (In collaboration with C. E. Prichard.) Oxford, 1872.
Selected Letters of Pliny. (In collaboration with C. E. Prichard.) Oxford, 1882.
"The Diversity of Holy Scripture" (a Sermon), in Barry's *Six Sermons on the Bible*. (1892.)
The Path to Freedom. (Five Sermons on Galatians.) Nisbet, 1894.
The English Sunday. (1903.)
Great Moral Teachers. (1906.)
Notes on the Table of Lessons for Holy Days. (1918.)
The Atonement. S.P.C.K. (1921).
Articles in Smith's *Dictionary of the Bible*.
Articles in Hastings's *Bible Dictionary*.

SERMONS

I. FLATTERY

I. Thess. ii. 5. *Neither at any time used we flattering words.*

There is a good deal of life and conduct which comes more under the head of manners than religion, at least in common estimation. And yet it is really all of it more or less in connexion with Christian principle and motives. That is the source from which it is to be renewed and purified when it becomes tainted from the world without. Such things as respect for our superiors in age and position, or freedom from self-consciousness and egotism, may appear to be simply good manners. But even allowing, which we do not, that this is all that can be said of them, are not good manners themselves a part of Christian life? It is when they come out of that source that they are most genuine, and then they please, even if they have not had that guidance and development which experience and contact with society can give.

Now there is a fault in personal intercourse which St Paul disclaims in the text, and one on which people generally look rather indulgently. In its lesser forms it is regarded merely as a fault of manners, or a want of good taste. But it is a fault which St Paul thinks serious enough to deny very emphatically, even when he is engaged with what appear to us charges of quite a different kind, charges of uncleanness, deceit, and covetousness. It is the sin of flattery which he disclaims. "Neither at any time used we flattering words." This is the only mention of flattery in the New Testament. But it is spoken of several times in the Old Testament. Its dangers did not escape the notice of those acute observers of life and character to whom we owe the sayings which form the Book of Proverbs. I will be content to quote one passage: "A flattering mouth worketh ruin".

It appears at first to be a very venial fault. There is so much to be said for it. It comes out of kindly feeling. It seems as if it would be harsh and ungrateful to condemn it. Yes, it is sometimes the overflowing of kindly feeling, but not always. However, allow that this is its source and character. It is not justified by that. In the first place it not seldom goes beyond truthfulness; it is not your candid, honest estimate of the person to whom you speak. You say more than you can say with truth. It may be quite unpremeditated untruth. You did not mean to go so far. But when once you begin, you are inevitably carried on. The sentence must be finished, and finished gracefully.

Again, granting this kindly intention in flattery, there is another point which may be noticed in it. It is meant to please, and that is to be its excuse. But does not the flatterer, whether consciously or not, look a little farther than that? Does he not try to please for the sake of being himself considered pleasant? If it be so, there is after all something of a personal aim in his flattery, when he appears to be merely saying kind things out of the kindness of his heart.

There is yet another accusation to bring against the fault, and it is much the most serious one. It is this: that it may do serious harm to the person flattered. I do not say that much harm will be done by it, when it only comes once and again. But when it comes often, when it comes from someone near at hand, when there are not one or two but many who flatter; then any man who is not thoroughly on his guard will be likely to suffer. You feed people again and again with this unwholesome food, and you create a desire for it where it never existed before. They come in some measure to accept your estimate of them. The conviction which they had of their own folly and weakness becomes obscured. Their very sense of sin as before God is damaged, and becomes a dogma rather than a present conviction. Different language, such as they hear from others, sounds ill-natured, and is so considered and treated by them. The work of honest friends, who used to help them by frank conversation, is made impossible. It is thus that a flatterer worketh, not ruin indeed, but damage, even serious damage, to good men. And yet nothing was farther from the intention of those whose fault it is, and if they were at all able to realise the consequences, they would be sincerely grieved.

It will perhaps be said that it is a person's own fault if he is affected by flattery, and that no good man or woman would be affected by it, because they know themselves too well. Unfortunately this is not the case. We are almost all susceptible to it in some degree. For instance, let someone appeal to what he calls our well-known philanthropy, generosity, and interest in good works. We are conscious that this is flattery, but we find, with a certain inward amusement, that we are more disposed to consider such an appeal. Some susceptibility to flattery on some side of our nature is true of almost all of us. There is some particular form of it which will succeed, if other and commoner forms repel and even disgust us.

Are we then never to praise others? Will not this strictness be the means of checking two good genuine human impulses—one of them, natural enthusiasm for human worth, and the other, natural gratitude for services received? No, for to praise and thank is not flattery, if praise be not to a man's face, and if it keep within the limits of truth. Flattery goes beyond the limits of truth, and disregards the modesty of those to whom it is addressed. Let us continue to speak warmly and heartily of human worth, let us show our thankfulness to those who have helped or served us. But let us remember that there is a modesty in good men which is to be considered and reverenced, and which indeed should be treated as if it existed, even where it does not. And let us not forget the constant danger of being carried by our feelings over the boundary of truth into the perilous realm of flattery.

Hitherto we have been considering what may by comparison be called disinterested flattery. But this is not flattery as understood by the authors of the Book of Proverbs, or by the old Greek philosophers, Plato,

Aristotle, and the rest, who have something to say on this matter. The proper idea of flattery is flattery with an object in view. It is spoken to get or gain something, influence, power, or gifts. Such flattery as that would be far from the minds of those whom we have hitherto been thinking of. It might seem unnecessary even to mention it to you. But it is not unnecessary. There is this sort of flattery, not in novels only, but in real life. These things actually happen. A woman attaches herself to another woman weaker and richer than herself. She does it for her own advantage. By flattery she obtains such a control over her, that her friend or her mistress, as the case may be, puts her means at her disposal, and is really in her hands. Or, again, a man uses such flattery to a woman that she is ensnared, and in his power. It is not likely that persons engaged in schemes so base would attend to any appeal that could be addressed to them here. But there is an initial stage in all these things, in which a person is just beginning to be led by Satan into a course of action which will develop into such schemes, and is hardly aware what he or she is meditating. To such persons I do appeal; and it is of use to do so. Are you using flattery to gain ends with such or such a friend, however small the matters may be which you are at present trying to get? If so, you are entering on a downward course. It is a course in which sensitiveness to truth and honour disappears, selfishness and cruelty begin to grow apace, and Conscience sleeps as if it were dead.

It would be easy to extend what has been said above,

and to apply it in other ways. There is flattery in politics. This was the sphere in which the Greek philosophers especially observed it. And it must always be one of the great dangers of a democratic government, whether at Athens or in England. Political leaders will flatter the electors in order to get place and power for themselves. There is flattery in the world of letters and art. No doubt there is plenty of severe, unkindly criticism, but there is also a good deal of the opposite kind, utterly unwarrantable and exaggerated praise, given in the spirit of flattery, because the writer or artist belongs to the critic's own school or coterie, or because there are personal ends to be gained by it.

But let me return to that disinterested and less culpable flattery which we were considering at first. We as Christians want to go to the root of the matter. Whatever is amiss in our lives, we want to deal with it, not superficially, by removing blemishes and improving our character externally. No, we set before ourselves afresh the likeness of Christ, and endeavour to grow up into Him in all things, to the measure of His stature. There has, we can see, been some neglect here and there of the balance of the Christian character. The love, kindliness, and gentleness which the Gospel breathes everywhere have had their effect. But the strong sense of truth which is no less inherent in the Gospel story, the fearless expression of it, which we read of, the courage to speak words which will offend and disappoint, these features have perhaps not affected us enough. How clear they are to see in Jesus in His converse with the multitude and with His disciples!

6

Things are expected of us, and that appears to be a reason for saying and doing them. Did Jesus always say and do what was expected of Him? How often we read the contrary! I do not mean that the Lord went about blaming men. He expressly repudiates this: "I came not to judge the world, but to save the world". Yet on the other hand He did not go about to praise. He could indeed say, "Be of good cheer" to those who needed it. They were many then, and they are many still. But He did not come to flatter men, He came to save them, and the two are incompatible. Think a little while about that incompatibility.

St Paul follows his Master. He also knew how to cheer and encourage. He does it abundantly in his Epistles, especially at the beginning of them. But yet he could say, "Neither used we at any time flattering words". We cannot make any such broad assertion, but we can endeavour to follow his example. It will often cost us an effort, and seem churlish. But we shall have our reward in the greater worth which will attach to our good word, in the greater help which it will give when spoken, in an influence for good not diminished but increased tenfold.

II. POPULARITY

Luke vi. 26. *Woe unto you when all men shall speak well of you.*

The condition described in the text comes nearer than anything else in the New Testament to the modern

7

conception of popularity. "Woe to you when you are popular," would be a fair equivalent for its meaning. Popularity is one of those seeming virtues which the world at large puts into competition with the sterner and severer virtues of the Christian faith. It has come to be considered that to say, a person is popular, is a high recommendation, and no words occur more commonly in testimonials. There never was a time when popularity met with more respect and recognition. In our schools and colleges, in our various professions, in society, in public life, this is what is admired and desired. Perhaps, then, it will be right for us to examine the claims of popularity in the light of the New Testament. The Gospel for the day[1] has a passage which certainly throws some suspicion on a wide and general popularity: "If ye were of the world, the world would love his own". But the text which I have taken is more explicit. There the claims of popularity are distinctly challenged, and that by the Lord Himself, "Woe unto you when all men shall speak well of you".

It must of course be acknowledged that the goodness or badness of popularity must depend in some degree on the character of the circle in which it is felt, of the people among whom it is enjoyed. The circle referred to in the text is that which then surrounded and was afterwards to surround the disciples of Jesus; in the first place the Galilean multitude and the hostile Jews. Popularity with the latter who rejected the Lord would of course mean unfaithfulness to their Master. So in our own day there may be circles, and tracts of

[1] St Simon and St Jude.

society, popularity in which would at once go against a man's character as a Christian, and others in which on the contrary it might rightly make us think well of him.

But the text appears to be widely intended. It says, "when *all* men shall speak well of you". And we may fairly interpret it as going beyond immediate circumstances and warning us of the dangers of popularity in general at all times and in all states of society. We may fairly interpret it as meaning that popularity is a danger to the spiritual life of those who possess it, and that, so far from its being at once accepted as a good sign with regard to the person who enjoys it, it may very well be the contrary, and imply a disposition and a course of conduct which are not according to the Divine standard.

Let us take the second of these two considerations. Is it probable that a life lived by a high religious standard will be popular? Are there not in many businesses, and in many households, ways and customs which make life easier, and depart just a little from the Christian standard of kindness, industry, truth, and honesty? Will not a thorough and simple endeavour to do all things as in God's sight, necessarily come into conflict with these ways? Is an unfailing adherence to truth, justice, and purity that which commends a man to the world at large or to any of the smaller worlds of our own wherein our life is passed, whether of school, college, society, or municipal life, even when those round us are for the most part, and on the whole, a good sort of people?

Such adherence may in time win respect. Attractive

personal qualities on the surface, where they exist, may go far to turn this respect into a moderate popularity. But this is a slow, uncertain process compared with the rapid, immediate popularity of those who, possessing the same qualities, have no such high standard and merely suit themselves to their surroundings.

Then, to take the other consideration mentioned above, there is the danger to the religious life of the person who is popular. There is of course the obvious danger of coming to think highly of himself because others like him, and of losing that deep humility and abasement of soul without which it is impossible truly to approach God in prayer. But I wish to point out something less obvious. When once the grateful seductive air of popularity has been breathed, a man is strongly tempted to go further in the direction of seeking it. This becomes his motive of action. And he himself does not know how much it is motive. While not disregarding higher principle, the voice of conscience, the example of good men, and the Word of God, and perhaps believing that these still direct his life, he is unconsciously allowing the desire for popularity to be his real guide, to decide his action, to be with him at all seasons, and in all questions. And when a choice comes, as it must sometimes come, between what is right, and what will be popular, he has not courage for the sacrifice of that on which his heart has been set.

Perhaps some of you have been reading a Life of the Duke of Wellington which has lately been published. The character there described is not a perfect character, far from it. But it would be difficult to find in history a man more absolutely loyal to duty, more entirely devoted to the service of his king and his country, more completely uninfluenced by the common desire for popularity. It was a matter of indifference to him, he had made it a matter of indifference, what people said or might say of him, what people thought or might think. It is in his political life that this disregard of popularity comes out most strongly. He may have been mistaken at times, indeed he was undoubtedly wrong in his judgments more than once, as we can see in the light of subsequent events. But his one animating principle was, what ought he to do, what did duty demand of him, duty to king and country? His own reputation for consistency, the goodwill of his personal friends and political associates were entirely disregarded. His conduct amazed and perplexed those who knew him best. There seemed to be no explanation. But the explanation was his sense of duty. How could he best serve his master? Does not all this suggest something to us in our capacity as Christians as well as in our capacity as subjects? Is the explanation of our conduct always to be found when it is regarded as simple endeavour how best to serve our Master?

There is another lesson to be learned from the same great character, the lesson of truthfulness. It is part of the same determination of mind, and can only fully exist where there is a disregard of popularity. The Duke's biographer dwells, and with good reason, on his fearless, unqualified truthfulness, publicly and to individuals, and his impatience of all equivocation. There is a special danger to truthfulness where popularity is an object, or where, to put it in a veiled phrase, a man has a care for his reputation. Slight deviations from and obscurations of truth relieve so much friction where many people have to be dealt with. The worldly view exactly inverts St Paul's teaching and practically bids us to be untruthful because we are "members one of another". It is only the man who habitually puts away from himself the aim of popularity who will be able always to be truthful. A really truthful man must often be unpopular, even where his truthfulness is truth spoken in love, with consideration, patience, and sympathy, and with a desire not to offend. Human nature among ourselves is very much what it was in the Galatian people, and we have to say what St Paul said to them: "Am I therefore become your enemy because I tell you the truth?"

But to return to the main subject. The danger of popularity is that it means the temptation of a secondary aim encroaching on and interfering with the straight course of Christian duty. Are we conscious of any such encroachment in however small a measure? We have taken for our help an inspiring example from among ourselves. But it is an example which will not commend itself to all. There is in it a tinge of severity and pride. Let us take a higher one, above ourselves. Can we use the word "popularity" in reference to the work and ministry of the Lord Jesus Christ? There was a period early in His ministry in which the Galilean multitude surrounded and acclaimed Him, but you know how He met those demonstrations, how He withdrew Himself from them, how the presence of those crowds only called forth from Him words which bid them count the cost of following Him, and were almost equivalent to a repulse. Looking back on His life He says: "If the world hate you, ye know that it hated me before it hated you". The indifference of our Saviour to popular favour was not indifference to the real love of human hearts. That was what He came to win, that was what refreshed Him, and refreshes Him still even at the right hand of God. So His example is not one which forbids to seek and value affection, if we seek it as He sought it, and value it next after His.

In conclusion let us nerve ourselves not to be led away by this prevailing folly, for such it is. Almost everything in modern life favours the value which is set upon popularity. Our representative system is one of the great encouragements of it. Popularity is not merely what causes a man to be elected, but it is constantly urged as a reason why you should elect him. To a thinking man it suggests a presumption that such a person will not have that firmness and simplicity of purpose which public life especially needs. Popularity is not a virtue, for in the first place, it is not part of the man himself, but something outside him, consisting in the feeling of others; and in some cases, it may be the sign of a life without settled principle, and moreover a cause of moral danger to the possessor of it.

Esteem, respect, affection, if they come, are to be treasured and valued as incentives to faithful work, to yet more faithful work than hitherto. These we may have, if God thinks well to give them to us. We have not now to choose between popularity and persecution as men have had to do in more trying times, and may have to do again. Yet if that choice has to be made in any measure let us remember the trenchant contrast which our Lord has drawn for us: "Woe unto you when all men shall speak well of you": "Blessed are ye, when men shall hate you, and cast out your name as evil, for the Son of man's sake".

III. ON PLEASING GOD

II. Cor. v. 9. *We labour, that, whether present or absent, we may be accepted of Him.*

We *labour* to please Him. Let us get rid at once of the word "labour". It clouds over a prospect which is really seen as bright. It introduces the thought of painful despondent effort. That is not St Paul's frame of mind. It is one of eager hopeful endeavour. It is our *ambition*, he says, to please Him. St Paul tells us precisely what his objects of ambition are. It is not every one who can afford to be so frank. They are *two*; to please Christ, and to preach the Gospel where it has not been preached before.

It is true that no stress can be laid on the strict rendering "we are ambitious". In the first place it is *not* a strict rendering. Our word "ambition" keeps something of the base associations of its Latin original and is a poor representative of the nobler φιλοτιμία.

But further, the Greek word itself has lost its special colouring and has come to mean *any* eager striving, not a striving for *distinction*. That indeed is the most eager form of pursuit known to higher minds, and is therefore employed for the aims of St Paul.

Yet there is more to be said than this. The histories of the word and of the man who uses it are parallel. They illustrate each other. Human affections are capable of being diverted like the words which express them, and retain their vividness when they have changed their aim.

Our affections can be diverted into new activities. It is indeed a thing that we shrink from attempting to do ourselves, and wisely. The shrinking is a warning of nature, and there is danger for those who disregard it. Human affections and aspirations are like great rivers. Much toil, vast expenditure, will do nothing to make them change their course. They recur to their channel in a night, and the labour is lost. But just as some uncalculated natural cause will effect completely and permanently what man's labour could not do, so it is with the diversion of our affections. Events, sudden or gradual, will do for us what we could not do for ourselves, and the stream of feeling and effort will roll on with the same power and volume in a direction whither we could not have believed it would tend. It would be easy to illustrate this from other affections, but we need not go beyond ambition. Ambition is *checked* by a religious career deliberately adopted as a calling. One sees plainly enough that theoretically at least there is no room for it there. But the eagerness of aim in life remains. It is diverted. What becomes of it? Does it merely change colour into an ecclesiastical or religious ambition? Is it working unacknowledged, and asserting itself more and more in the inward struggle of motives? We trace the signs of it in others, but what enables us to do so is that we know the signs of it in ourselves.

Or does this eagerness of aim take a fresh course *altogether* and become an eager striving to please our Master? That was St Paul's history. His was a religious ambition to begin with. It was probably never anything else, vehement as it was. A Jew had little scope for anything else. That then was not the new direction with him, a religious in place of a secular ambition. His passion ran into the current expressed in the text: "*My* aim is to please Him". His ambition was transformed, as his glorying was transformed. That glorying or proud exultation in what he had or was or could do, which was one of the most marked features of his character—we know what became of it. It left the privileges of pure Jewish blood, the glories of the nation, the perfect fulfilment of the law on which it had rested. It did not venture to dwell on sufferings and achievements. It paused on his children in the Gospel, and their salvation by his means, but it rested nowhere finally except in the Cross of the Lord Jesus Christ.

I dwell on St Paul not merely because the words of the text are his words, but because we cannot do without him in this matter. It is because ambition did, as a fact, undergo this transformation in him that we can speak of it as possible for ourselves. We have in him a man whose life and character, as they lie *so* open before us, were plainly lived as he says they were, to please *Him*. Could the Christian character ever have been realised if we had not had the record of St Paul's heart? Could we have understood what it was to be, could we have ventured to attempt it as a possible thing in its singleness and devotion and diversion of affections? What St Paul did for Christian doctrine by his thought is evident enough both to friends and foes. It is perhaps not so evident what he did for Christian life by *his* life. And yet this was the greatest side of his work.

But it must be confessed that in us ambition does not undergo this transformation easily and readily. It remains, as has been long since pointed out in this pulpit, in the man with a religious career, as religious ambition. And there is another strange phase of it. Contrary to the whole tenor of our Lord's teaching, it has been thought spiritually-minded to cherish ambition as to honours and distinctions in the life to come. We hear little of such motives now, and it is well that it is so. Is it any wonder that ambition should prove so obstinate a factor in human character when we consider how earnestly it is stimulated at all places of education, and not least at our Universities? Can we expect a man to go out into civil life and to make it his first object to serve God in his generation, or to serve his country or his clients or his dependents, if up to that moment we have pressed on him by every means in our power that the first thing for him to do was to obtain distinction for himself, with the bye-consideration that the distinction would reflect some of its lustre on the body to which he belonged? Can we not see here some explanation of the evident prevalence of *personal* aims in the public men of our day? Again, can we expect one of our students thus educated to put this habit of mind wholly aside on entering a distinctly religious career?

Of course the stimulus cannot be dispensed with under present conditions and it is difficult even to *imagine* conditions seriously different. But it is well to keep in mind the radical fault of a system depending so largely on love of distinction, when it is taken as a preparation for life in the service of the State, or of the Church. Those who respond most keenly to the stimulus are perhaps by their very nature also most capable of seeing its deficiencies if fairly set before them.

Is there anything better, any substitute? There is only one thing better, and that is so difficult, so distant. We make it *our aim* to please *Him*.

What is the one great difficulty of this transmuted ambition? It is that, as the text says, "we are absent from the Lord".

"Whether present or absent", St Paul says. It made no difference to him. But it does make a great difference to us. To please a present Master is a motive which all would allow as sufficient. Ambition as a motive for public service would disappear under His eye. He would be felt to draw all regards. And much more would this be the case in His immediate service, the service of His Church. We should be able to do what we wish to do now, to do everything for Him. So we *imagine*. But is not all this mere imagining, and may not our present trial of service by faith be really more merciful than a trial of service by sight?

However, we do not think so. The drawback is so obvious. There is no *sign* of how He takes what we do. An eager desire, eager by its very hypothesis, which has to fill the place of an eager passion for distinction, is to pursue its aim indefatigably through a long life without the possibility of meeting with any recognition or assurance. That is what we embark in, when we make it *our* aim to please *Him*.

But this is not quite an accurate account of the matter. We do find indirect assurances of our acceptance (1) in the opinion of men, and (2) in our own consciousness. First, suppose we meet with gratitude and confidence from those we deal with. *Here* is an assurance that we are pleasing Him. His blessing has evidently been with us in our work, of whatever kind that work may have been. This gratitude and confidence would not have been earned without it. Can it be that although *not* pleased with us, He has nevertheless been using and blessing us as mere indifferent instruments in His hand? We may be sure that His love does not so play with human souls as if they were dead things. By this gratitude and this confidence which are so sweet to us He is conveying His approval, and we may take them in that way. No doubt the inference is illogical. You may sternly renounce it in the supposed interest of truth. But it will come back and press itself upon you, and I believe it is a message from *Him*.

Yet how much danger there is in looking for it too anxiously. We soon begin to seek it *directly* for its *own sake*, and when that is done, it ceases to be a message. Again, not only do we lose the higher motive and the close relation with the Lord which it implies, but a wholly different process at once sets in, in the moulding of our character. A life to please the Lord moulds us slowly and surely on His pattern. A life to please men, even good men, moulds us on an inferior pattern. Weaknesses, errors of judgment, ignorances, faults which were perhaps not considerable in *them* must come out again in those who live to please them, even if that pleasing be concerned with their real good and conceived in a high spirit. The proverb says "The disciple shall be as his master", but there is also truth in the converse—the master shall be as his disciple, if the master's aim is to please the disciple.

Secondly we find an assurance that we are pleasing Him in our own consciousness. It reports an access of peace and hope, a sense of spiritual sunshine. This we believe is imparted by *Him*. It is, according to St John, so distinctly an object of spiritual intuition as to constitute a proof to us of something else, namely that our prayers are answered. "Whatsoever we ask, we receive of Him, because we keep His commandments, and do the things that are pleasing in His sight."

Yet we know too well the precariousness of such intuitions. If this joy in the sense of pleasing Him is directly imparted, what are we to say of spiritual distress and depression? Are they signs that we have not been pleasing Him, or is it often truer to say of these, "It is mine own infirmity"—an expression too apt for our purpose to be passed over, however inaccurate it may be as a translation? Spiritual depression often does not mean anything more than physical weakness, or at most a temporary weakness of faith. It does not mean that God has forgotten to be gracious or shut up His lovingkindness in displeasure. If we urge as a topic of consolation that depression may be purely subjective, is it not honest to own that *exultation* may be so as well? Thus it may be pleaded that the sense of acceptance may arise from an opposite kind of infirmity. But it can never be an infirmity, for a soul which desires God, to believe and to rejoice in His love. This is the *health* of the soul.

There is a danger no doubt in building too much on particular frames of mind. Even when some real sacrifice has been made which is plainly according to His will, when the sense of its acceptance is all the stronger because it has failed of its immediate and earthly object, even then we shall be wise if we taste sparingly and almost tremblingly of the assurance that we have pleased Him. And yet there is assurance. It is possible of course to regard every mental phenomenon as merely subjective; but that is not Christianity. Is this then to be our object in life, to please Him, and to have nothing to look to here but these phantom assurances, as the sceptic will certainly consider them to be? See, he says, what abundant objects life presents. Can we substitute for them, in their nearness, colour, and potency, something so distant and unrecognisable? Now Doubt does not always hold this language about the abundance of sufficient aims in life. But it is true that they lie round the young in sufficient profusion. What are we to do with these aims? Can we keep them in the front and relegate the aim of *pleasing Him* to a nominal headship in the background? No, it must be in the front, and we must see all other aims through it. Then we shall see them in their true colour and proportion.

But such a life is a heroic life if not a quixotic one. We want a life which will suit the average mass of mankind who are not heroes. It is true that Christianity is essentially a heroism. And that is just why it is adapted to the mass of mankind. There are in every man possibilities of heroism. They may only show themselves in the passive form of admiring the heroism of others, but they can be called out, and this is what Christianity does. Very commonplace and grotesque are the forms which the heroism will sometimes take, but it is heroism. Yet again there are some whose concern in this matter is largely for others. Can I send out a young man into the world with such an aim as this to guide him, to please one so distant, so mysterious, so irresponsive? Certainly we cannot, unless we find that aim sufficient for ourselves, unless it is, *in purpose at least*, our own supreme aim. But it *is* sufficient. More and more He fills the sky of our mental view. His space and share in our thought and hope grow larger as the years advance, not so much because we draw nearer to Him as Judge but because He is more with us as Saviour. We *know* that we need not hesitate to put this aim before them. Perhaps they will fasten on it at once, instead of drawing to it as we have done ourselves with the lapse and loss of years.

But, is it *possible* to please God? May not the aim be not only difficult and distant, but altogether out of reach? Is it possible on the human side, and is it possible on the Divine? Had we not better restrict ourselves to the more guarded phrase, "Keep His commandments", and abandon the spontaneity, freedom, and interest of so incautious an expression as *pleasing God*?

And first, is it possible from the human side? An exaggerated view of human depravity formerly cast its injurious shadow over all endeavour, even the endeavours of those who were not in the flesh but in the spirit. But theology no longer delights to draw out the logical consequences of Scripture phrases on the sinfulness of man apart from the qualifications supplied by parallel lines of thought also running through Scripture. Few English Churchmen would now hold the exaggerated language which used to be held about human action, even when guided by Grace. But traces of the same downcast spirit linger still among us; we need bolder thoughts of how surely and truly we can please God if we are enabled by His grace. Consider the sight of a good man steadily fixing his desire on serving his Master, sacrificing present good to it, striving with himself, beaten and returning to the endeavour, and all this by faith, without any sensible mark to encourage him. How must this appear in the sight of Him for Whom it is done, by Whose grace it is done? Do the faults and failures neutralise the moral beauty of the effort, or do they only make it more pathetic? It is perhaps dangerous to guess how things appear in God's sight, but something like this seems implied in the conception of Him as our Father. From the human side it is possible to please God.

But is it possible from the Divine side? Can God be pleased? The Psalmist says, "The Lord's *delight* is in them that fear Him, in them that wait for His mercy". And the word which describes the Lord's pleasure in His people runs through the whole range of the Old Testament. Are we to dismiss this expression along with others as anthropopathic? We *may* do so, no doubt. But there is a real danger in trying to get behind these conceptions. At any rate, they sum up and represent for us what we need to know, and if we insist on going behind them we shall find ourselves in empty space, no wiser, no nearer the truth, on the contrary farther from it, and—infinitely poorer.

But happily the matter is perfectly clear for us. We are concerned with God in Christ, God manifest in the flesh. The anthropopathic expressions of the Old Testament (not of course all of them, but such as that we are dealing with) are literally true of Him. He can be pleased. He is not in His human nature impassible; this phrase of pleasing Him is not a cover for something inscrutable. He is pleased with me and my efforts to honour and serve Him just as I am pleased and touched by the loving acts of those who are close and dear to me. Nothing is too *small* to escape Him if it be done in love and simplicity. He can be pleased. I can please Him. It is a *childish* view of religion. But of such children is the Kingdom of God.

IV. UNITY OF AIM

Phil. iii. 13. *One thing I do.*

How unlike this is to the case of most of us! Instead of having one thing to do, we have many things, which jostle each other, and leave us no room and no time to concentrate ourselves. Take a common case. A man is in business. He has all its various calls to attend to. He has also family cares, perhaps anxious ones. He has public, and social duties, and moreover private tastes and interests quite remote from these. He is sometimes ready to say, "Happy are those who have only one thing to do. They can concentrate their powers and do the one thing well. I can do nothing thoroughly". Yet we know or ought to know the immense value of variety. There are dull monotonous lives in which there is no variety, in which if not the same things, yet the same routine goes on day by day. How gladly some of them would share your multiplicity of interests! Instead of complaining, you should give thanks that you have many things to do.

But you have perhaps a deeper and better grounded reason for wishing for more unity in your life. You are sensible of other aims present at times to your conscience, if not pursued: the deliverance of your soul from sin and guilt and judgment, restraint of passions, and victory over temptation, spiritual progress, doing some good in the world, making some use of life, relieving suffering, and redeeming the time. These things also you either do or wish to do. Not only are they separate aims from those which we at first enumerated, but in some respects they appear opposed to them. There is an actual conflict, in some instances, between the one and the other. Again you say, "Happy are those who have unity of purpose in their lives, as for instance the clergy, whose business these things are, with which my business conflicts. The clergy can say, or ought to be able to say, 'One thing I do'. This is what is set them, to do good and to be good. A clergyman has nothing to turn him aside. His path is straight, he has no distractions as I have". This indeed is not quite true, but the thought is a natural one and deserves an answer. We will pass over lesser and reasonable objections and take wide ground. The answer is this. Unity of aim in life is not to be sought by fixing on one aim and excluding all others, even if that one aim be God's service in the ministry of the Church. It is attained rather by fixing on one aim, which will by its nature include and contain the rest as subordinate. And so it follows that the clerical life, in which other aims are, ideally, put aside, is not essentially better than the layman's life, in which they remain in full activity, but are, ideally, subordinated to and unified by the supreme aim, God's will and God's glory, to be recognised and sought in every kind of work. If we can form that habit of thought, and obtain that view it will give unity to the life which we live, unity not by excluding all but one, but by including all.

How are we to seek and form this habit of thought? Not necessarily by outward profession, by putting forward in words that we do all to the glory of God. And yet although we shrink from such language in connexion with the common duties of life when people use it too freely, there are nevertheless those from whom we know that it comes quite naturally, and is the merely unrestrained expression of what they actually feel. Then if we be ourselves in earnest, we shall feel that it edifies us, even though we could not so speak ourselves without putting force on our natural bent. But the religious aim in dominion over life is better sought by speaking of it to God than by speaking to man, and it is by prayer that it is gained. That prayer without ceasing, of which St Paul speaks, is not the impossible task of a continuous utterance of petitions, but a mind which often relapses naturally, or shall we say by Grace, into a praying frame, which desires, waits, and expects continually some Divine blessing or some Divine acceptance of what is being done. There is nothing which we have to do which we may not so consecrate by prayer. "In that day", says Zechariah speaking of the Messianic times, "there shall be on the bells of the horses, Holiness unto the Lord." There shall be no difference between holy and profane. Everything whatever its use will be dedicated to God, and He will be remembered in it.

Thus we find an answer to the demand for unity in life, and yet even now not a sufficing one. Even now, while fixing your mind by prayer on religious aims, you feel a want of unity in them also. There seem to be various aims in this sphere also. There is the salvation of my own soul which I am bid to work out in fear and trembling; there is also the formation of character and the eradication of faults; the stewardship of gifts and capacities entrusted to me. Again there is, as was said just now, the glory of God to be sought, and the extension of His Kingdom; and on the other hand there is the service of man, and a life to be lived for the good of others. Which am I to attend to? I want unity, one thing to which all effort may be directed. I am weak and wavering. Give me unity. Enable me to say with St Paul, "One thing I do". I think the answer will run thus. All these aims which you distinguish from one another, and seem to hesitate among, are but different aspects of the one thing which you desire to find. If they seem different to you, it is because they are as yet only names to you, and conceptions, known to thought and reason, but very little to experience. As soon as you follow, seek, and lay hold of any of them, you will find that they run up into one. If you seek to serve God, you will find yourself engaged in the service of men. If you seek for the salvation of your soul, you will find that you are striving after holiness of life. Honestly follow up the one aim from any side and you will find no distractions, no division of energy, much less conflict of purpose. If only you start from faith in Jesus Christ and His Gospel, all these views and aspects are but ways in which salvation in His name attracts you and opens itself to you, in which it puts itself before different minds in different phases. At one time it is good for you to be seeking peace and forgiveness, at another to strive to glorify Him among men, at another to seek to know Him, at another to labour in the service of your fellow-men. But the aim is really one, all achieved in one power, faith in Jesus Christ and His help. In all you will be able to say, "One thing I do".

And this aim is not only one in itself notwithstanding its many aspects, but it can also give unity to all your life. If you can get it definitely established in your habit of thought, it will tell on all the rest, and gradually subordinate them to itself. Then when that is so, the subordinate temporary purposes of life may fail one by one but the main purpose of life cannot fail or be disappointed. That is part of its character. It will be carried out. Where it is, life cannot be a failure.

This then is what we want to do. But it is necessary to recognise that it is exactly the opposite of this which often happens. Instead of our religion giving unity to other aims, they intrude into our religious life and destroy its unity and simplicity. Perhaps some thoughts on this matter will not be unsuitable to my text. With some of us what is wanted is not so much to detect and convict and overcome sins plainly outside a good life and contrary to it, as to attend to the defects and diseases which belong to the Christian life itself. Let us turn our observation to these.

The aim of gain gets into religion. It is not that men deliberately "suppose that godliness is a way of gain", but their actions sometimes lie that way. Perhaps it is common in the pulpit to speak in a hard, contemptuous way of this inclination. A poor woman comes to church regularly and it is partly in the hope of getting material relief. But the speaker who condemns this so strongly has not himself known the pressure of poverty out of which such inclination comes. When it is a tendency arising straight out of bitter, painful necessities, it deserves to be dealt with in pity and sympathy, not in contempt. But many men who have little excuse know the danger and they should ask themselves, "Do I in my religious activities of whatever kind allow the thought of worldly advancement to stimulate me?" When we are clear ourselves in such respects as this, we can understand and deal with the temptations of the poor.

Then there is the aim of being liked. The desire of pleasing society gets into our religion. There are of course times and places where a religious life is not the way of finding favour, but there are times and places where it is. There never was a day in which the desire of being liked had so strong a power as it has now. That this should be so has its good side, it is a sign of greater solidarity and brotherhood. But it intrudes where it has no business to come. Does this desire inwardly guide and influence me, where apparently and professedly I am being guided by religious motives? It will be almost enough to make us earnest in dealing with the fault if we set it before us in its true colours. I am seeking to serve and please God in order that I may be acceptable to the society in which I live. There is also a third intrusive aim which may be mentioned—the aim of strengthening and advancing some particular form of ecclesiastical opinion, not necessarily extreme opinion, but one of the many various forms in which the truth appears to earnest minds. Believe me, this piety in order to promote a cause is a real danger. It may seem to be a religious motive, but if it be so at all it is a very mixed one. It mars the simplicity of religion, and comes in between the soul and God, and keeps them apart.

I am not recommending constant inquiry into motives. We shall only perplex and deceive ourselves if we attempt that. But seek simplicity and unity of aim. You will not fully attain to it, but be alive to and jealous of all that impairs it. Simplicity of purpose is what gives beauty and power to life. It outshines high station and intellectual gifts, and it gives grace to the obscure lives of the humble and the poor.

V. COMFORT

Ps. xciv. 19. P.B.V. *Thy comforts have refreshed my soul.*

There is a little book written five hundred years ago by one Thomas of Kempen, which is I suppose more or less known to many of us. Its title is *Of the Imitation of Christ.* It was written in the first instance for the novices and monks of the convent to which he belonged, and its original purpose and limitations must be borne in mind by those who read it. But it has characteristics which have given it an infinitely wider range, and have placed it in the first rank of Christian books of devotion. There are three distinct regions of spiritual experience in which this book can help us. Do we need to bring down to the dust that good opinion of ourselves which the world has fostered and our position in it has encouraged in us? Humility is hardly a strong enough word to express the utter sense of frailty, inconsistency, and unworthiness which runs through all the prayers, meditations, and thanksgivings of the book. Contempt and despite of self may seem extravagant words, but the humility is so simple and sincere that it cannot fail to touch us. If this be the true mind of so good a man, what am I in the sight of God?

Then there is Thomas's entire detachment from worldly aims and possessions. Here of course he speaks from monastic ground. But I suppose there is not one of us who does not at times feel a desire for some greater measure of detachment. It comes to us all in face of death, but we want to have it while we live. We must live in the world, but we want not to be wholly and simply of the world.

Thirdly there lies before us in this book what Thomas himself dares to call "the familiar friendship of Jesus", a secret close communion with Jesus, represented in question and answer, in prayer and inward response to prayer. Happy shall we be if we are led to seek for something like it. Thomas was a mystic, and this communion with the Saviour belongs to his mysticism, but it is a practical mysticism in harmony with Scripture.

I could not forbear asking your attention at the outset to these three characteristics of this famous book, closely related as they are to one another in ways which I must not now pause to explain. But my purpose in mentioning the *De Imitatione* is to bring forward quite another aspect of it, which will illustrate the text I have chosen, "Thy comforts have refreshed my soul", and at the same time has a special fitness for this Sunday, Refreshment Sunday as it is called. Throughout the book there is a topic which recurs again and again, pathetically, almost plaintively. It is the desire of refreshment, comfort, consolation—solace, if we may take the English equivalent of the Latin word in the original. The picture before us is a pathetic one, a human heart which has disclosed itself thoroughly to us, which we have got to know intimately, this human heart longing sorely for some comfort to soften the hardships of monastic life and refresh him in its dreariness. Yet none the less there is the fixed determination to reject all external solace as an obstacle to spiritual comfort and the solace of Divine grace. Here are his own words: "When a man attains to this, that he seeks not his comfort from any creature, then doth God first begin to be perfectly sweet to him".

And even this stern resolution does not contain the full severity of Thomas's attitude to the comfort which he so sorely needs. While the only solace he will admit is the inward consolation bestowed by God on the soul, yet even this he refuses to seek for eagerly, he is content to be deprived of it and not to grieve when it is withdrawn. He is afraid of loving Jesus because Jesus gives him solace. That would be a mercenary love. He thirsts for spiritual consolation, he has refused everything else to make room for it, all creature comforts and human society—but *inward* comfort is often withdrawn and he humbly submits.

We can admire the devotion and submission enshrined in such passages. We can fully agree that inward spiritual consolation is not to be sought for with too great eagerness, but waited for till it comes. But first of all we cannot help seeing that the utter rejection of all *external* solace is not God's purpose for us, still less a condition of His grace. Certainly we are meant to draw comfort from one another. Does not St Paul tell us how the faith alone of his converts refreshes his soul? Spiritual comfort given to one man is meant to be imparted to others. The weaker may help the stronger. Moreover the solace given to our physical nature, and so through it to the spirit, by the gift God has provided for our sustenance and bodily welfare, is to be received with thankfulness. And external nature with its sights and sounds was designed to have an influence of solace and consolation, such as we sometimes feel in the beauty of the early spring.

We can see that Thomas and the mystics go too far in requiring all other solace to be rejected as the condition of divine consolation, but it is none the less true that seeking refreshment continually from all other quarters does distract the mind and bring atrophy to our spiritual receptiveness for divine comfort.

34

But here I think we need to pause. Is it an adequate
view of religion that it consists in seeking and receiving spiritual comfort? That is a totally inadequate
view, and needs I think to be protested against. There
is much in religious literature, and especially in religious
poetry which seems to countenance this view. But
when Christ said, "Come unto Me and I will refresh
you", He added the words, "Take My yoke". The
Christian religion is not merely or primarily a method
of seeking spiritual comfort. It is something very
different. It is a definite courageous purpose of
obedience to the law of Christ contained in His words
and example, communicated to us by His Spirit, a
daily conflict with the world and the flesh, a daily submission of our will to the will of God, a perseverance
in spite of weak faith and moral failures, a life which,
to use the famous phrase of Origen, is one continuous
prayer. That such a life should from time to time
receive inward consolation, enjoy peace passing understanding, and be able to see all things around itself in
the light of God's love, this is a consequence which
follows, a gracious appointment, but not the essence
of religion. There is real need to emphasise this. Men
turn to religion for solace and comfort, and they do
not find it, either in the word or the sacrament. They
are ready to say, "Your promises are vain, we have
sought your *consolations and cannot find them*". We
must reply, "They are not to be found in this way.
First take the yoke, and then wait for the refreshment". Let us hear what Thomas says of spiritual
refreshment. "Lord, I am not worthy of Thy con-

solation or of any spiritual visitation. And therefore Thou dealest justly with me, when Thou leavest me poor and desolate." It is those who can speak thus to whom consolation comes. And if this be the true attitude of the believer, it is plain that he will not look on the measure of consolation granted to him as the measure of his spiritual state. Let me quote again; the words are the answer of Jesus. "All is not lost because at times thy heart is not stirred towards Me as thou wouldst have it be. Thou must not lean too much on that good and sweet affection which thou sometimes feelest."

In what form does consolation come? Best of all in a sense of the personal individual love of God for our own souls. Here there is always one great initial difficulty. I can believe that God Who is love, loves the world which He has made, and all the more because of the misery that is in it. Not to think so would be to conceive of God as less loving than we are ourselves. And the witness of His love is the Son of God upon the Cross. But when it comes to the individual, when the question is, "Can God love me such as I am, unfaithful, worldly, and vain?" it is a much harder matter to believe. Therefore we may say that if the sense of His love comes to us, it is not from within that the experience arises, it is His direct action on the soul. "The love of God is shed abroad in our hearts by the Holy Ghost which is given unto us." That this great consolation should not be always given us, is nothing wonderful. We are not capable of bearing it. Instead of being a blessing it would be a danger.

More often consolation comes by way of a quickened sense of some particular spiritual gifts. Pardon, grace, peace—how often these words pass our lips with little or no meaning! But when they are attached to definite circumstances in our lives, moments in which we wanted them and they came, we feel that here are gifts freely given to us, actual facts, on which we can look back with thankfulness, just as our human affections are refreshed when we take out some treasured letter or memento which reminds us of past acts of human friendship. From that sin God delivered me; in that difficulty God sustained me by His grace; after those doubts and fears He gave me peace. And here it is that we can gain so much from one another.

But consolation does not come only through a quickened sense of God's spiritual gifts, and quickened apprehension of His promises. It comes also through awakening to the love of God manifest in temporal blessings, in the gifts of friendship and affection which surround us and come from Him, in all the beauty of the world, which owes its power to soothe and charm us to the presence and glory of God which is in it. There is no side of our spiritual experience in which at the present day we feel so much need of solace as in respect of faith. We little know the struggle which sometimes goes on in earnest Christian hearts against doubt of the most comprehensive kind. Is there after all a God, a life beyond death? Cannot all the Christian creed be explained away as the creation of human fancy? It is for such needs that we want solace, the

37

solace which comes from the faith of others. There is something to help us in the silent fellowship of united worship for which we are met Sunday by Sunday; but how much more help would there be if we could at times break the reserve which closes our lips, and share the difficulties which beset, and the tokens which confirm, our faith. God will bless the effort. St Paul's hope in visiting the Roman Church was not to come as the inspired Apostle, but as the simple believer to gain as well as give. "I long to see you, that I with you may be comforted in you, each of us by the other's faith, both yours and mine."

And now, what have we arrived at? That the life of man, however prosperous outwardly, needs solace, and some lives need it most acutely. And that this solace, although it comes to us in many other ways, is nevertheless most effectual when it comes to us on our spiritual side. Yet it is not to be sought for in itself or for itself. That would be an effeminate conception of religion, and misleading in a hundred ways. What we have to do is to live the active Christian life in dependence on Divine strength and guidance, submitting our self-will to the will of God, and carrying on that inward conflict with our own passions and infirmities which will not cease till the end. As we go forward, solace will come to us when and how God will. We must not be discouraged for lack of it. But when it comes we humbly rejoice. We have in our heart, as the Psalmist says in this same verse, a multitude of thoughts, thronging, mingling and passing. But when the touch of Divine solace comes, the throng are silent and melt away. God speaks to us, and in the multitude of the thoughts which we have in our heart, His comforts refresh our soul.

VI. DEATH

Luke ii. 29. *Lord, now lettest Thou Thy servant depart in peace, according to Thy word.*

It will be worth our while to consider the words used in the New Testament to express death. When we speak of the death of a friend, we naturally incline to use some other gentler word. So did the saints of the New Testament. What were these other words?

1. To depart. So St Paul speaks of death. "Having a desire to depart and to be with Christ." The word in the original is full of metaphor. It is the word used of breaking up a camp, or unmooring a vessel. Here perhaps we may recognise the suggestion to which we owe Tennyson's *Crossing the bar.*

2. To go to rest, to fall asleep. So we read of St Stephen, "When he had said this he fell asleep". The contrast is no doubt intentional between the scene of cruel violence, and the peaceful entrance into repose.

3. There are other words which deserve examination, but we must go on to the text. In the passage before us from to-day's Gospel,[1] there is another word, quite distinct from those already mentioned, and containing a very special thought. It is this, death is release. "Lord, now dost Thou release Thy

[1] Presentation of Christ in the Temple.

servant according to Thy word, in peace." It is the word used in Greek for disbanding an army, for discharging a soldier, for relieving a sentry, for sending away a servant to rest.

It is then a word which recognises our true relation to God as His servants, and servants on duty, who cannot leave their post until released by their Master. It is worth noticing that the same Greek word is used in the Septuagint of one whose duty and life ended at the same moment, Aaron the priest (Num. xx. 29). So Simeon uses it as expressing what death seemed to be to him. His words are not, as is sometimes supposed, a prayer for release. He does not say, "Lord, now release Thy servant", but, "Lord, now Thou dost release Thy servant". It is a thankful acknowledgment, not a prayer. The canticle is known as *Nunc dimittis*, not *Nunc dimitte*.

Death regarded as a release: that then is our subject. Think of this, how strange and unusual an aspect of it. For most of us, to die would not be to be released, but rather to be torn away painfully from those whom we love most dearly, and from all our aims, employments, and present hopes. Yet we repeat these words of Simeon, constantly, perhaps daily.

It is true we have often seen sufferers who in their pain desire death as a release. But that is not the thought in the text. Here is a man who, though aged, is still vigorous. He comes into the temple, as you have come into church to-day. But Simeon has been serving and waiting with a special expectation. His Divine Master now bids him go and rest. The sign has come which tells him so. The expectation is fulfilled. He accepts the sign and rejoices in it.

Now there is something for us to learn from this view of death. This view of death implies a view of life very different from that which many of us have, namely, a view of life as active service, as labour, as being "on duty" in close relation to a Master, and all this in a way which certainly not all people realise. Apply this conception of death to the close of a life which has been simply one of ease and self-indulgence. How false to speak of such a person as being relieved like a soldier on duty, released from labour like a servant who has toiled all day. One hears the hymn sung, "Now the labourer's task is o'er", and yet the man's object in life has been to save himself all trouble, even in worldly things. He has been no labourer. Can you honestly offer thanks to the Heavenly Master for his relief and release? Is this an occasion for *Nunc dimittis*?

But take the life of active service which some are living, the service of God in serving man. This may be fulfilled in many different ways; but it has one characteristic which gives it unity. It is diligent, strenuous, fearful of wasting time or losing opportunity. It may meet with very different measures of success. It may be led under very trying circumstances, or under very happy and encouraging ones. But when death comes, you feel that the *Nunc dimittis* does belong to such a life. When such a person dies, the Lord is relieving and releasing His servant. I will not say, discharging him from service, for there is yet a service for him hereafter, "His servants shall serve Him".

Or again, take a life, not of active but of passive service, in which weakness, pain, or the infirmities of age are long endured. That also is service, though we may not yet see what the result is. There also, when death comes, it is a release.

Death is a release from service. Yet I do not mean that we must at all times, and at all stages of life be able so to regard it. Indeed we cannot. Most of us who are here have vigour for more service, and desire for more. We do not want to be released yet. Our interests are in the world, not the world in its bad sense, as something apart from God, but in human society and its duties, in human life and its pursuits. They are all good interests, capable of being made means for glorifying God. Simeon was an old man, and his words were spoken at the moment of a wonderful revelation, under the strong impulse which it gave. We are not at the end of the allotted span of life, but in the midst of it. We cannot use his words precisely as he did.

But the question still remains: Is our life such that we can reasonably expect that, when death comes near, we shall be able to use Simeon's words, or that others will be able to use them about us? Can we hope that, in any degree, we shall feel death to be a discharge from service faithfully performed according to our various conditions? Is that the character which our end will simply and naturally bear on the face of it, a release from faithful service in doing or suffering, or perhaps in both? That is what our use of the *Nunc dimittis* should, day by day, suggest to us.

But there is more than this in the text. It is a release of a particular kind. It is "according to Thy word, in peace" (R.V.). A release in peace, with anxieties stilled and desires satisfied; and this in accordance with God's word, that is, in accordance with a promise formerly given that they should be so stilled and satisfied. Simeon did not need a promise of release. Release was sure to come, it comes to all men; but a release in peace, that was a special matter. To some, peace in its completeness is revealed at the very moment of release; to some, not till after it; but for others, as for Simeon, it comes before. What was it that made Simeon's departure a departure in peace? It was that he departed with an amazing token of Divine favour. He has seen the Messiah, he has held in his arms the Glory of Israel and the Light of the Gentiles. We know nothing of Simeon's actual death. He may have died in bodily pain, as many do, but of this we are sure, it was a departure in peace.

Yet surely there is in some respects a greater assurance of peace for us, who know all that the Saviour has done, His Atonement, and Resurrection. For Simeon all this was still implicit, wrapped up in the Divine promises. It was a Babe that he took in his arms. He may have foreseen much by the spirit of prophecy. Indeed his words to Mary show that he did. But for us it lies before us clearly, not implicit, but in all completeness. As Simeon took the Babe in his arms, so we embrace and hold fast the blessed hope of everlasting life in the Person of Jesus Christ. To Simeon it came at the end of life. We have it all our lives. Yet perhaps, like him, we may look to see salvation clearer at the end.

In conclusion, let us notice how much at variance this idea of release from conflict, and discharge from service, appears to be with certain mediaeval teaching which is gaining ground in our Church. According to that teaching the release in peace is but the introduction to a long period of suffering and purgation for all the saved. How inconsistent the two conceptions are! How largely the latter annuls the reality of the former! Where can you find in Scripture anything which even hints at such a discipline? The passage in I. Cor. iii, which is sometimes quoted, has as you probably know an entirely different significance. Why should we, arguing simply from earthly experience, be ready to accept a doctrine nowhere taught in Scripture? Change, progress, completion, all this our moral and spiritual nature needs, but for these it will be sufficient to be with Christ. "We know that we shall be like Him for we shall see Him as He is."

VII. CHRIST PRESENT

John xvi. 28. *I leave the world.*
Matt. xxviii. 20. *I am with you alway.*

"When I feel age creeping on me", so said one who had done good service to his generation, "when I feel age creeping on me, and know that I must soon die—

I hope it is not wrong to say it—but I cannot bear to leave the world with all the misery in it." These broken emphatic words have a ring of genuineness. To some they may appear to savour of self-confidence, but the life's work which the speaker had done makes them, from his lips, simply truthful and natural. "I cannot bear to leave the world with all the misery in it."

No such saying is recorded of our Lord.

He dwells with calm joy on His return to the Father. He prays for His exaltation. "Glorify Me with the glory which I had before the world was." There are indeed sad anticipations of what must come after His departure, and affectionate care and prayer for those whom He leaves behind. But all this has narrow limits. It has regard to a small body of personal friends. We indeed have a right in virtue of our common faith to press into that body, and claim participation in every word of comfort, especially in the promise of the Spirit. But as to the vast misery of the world He says nothing, and nothing of any reluctance to leave it. This is His attitude. It is thus that He departs and ascends. His disciples accept it as what they expect, and after the Ascension they return to Jerusalem with great joy.

There is of course a sufficient answer to the contrast which has been suggested. It lies in the exultant words of St Paul: "He ascended far above all heavens that He might fill all things". He ascended, not that He might leave, but that He might *fill*. It was the beginning of a fuller, more pervading redemptive action. The Divine glory consists in the manifestation of the Divine attributes, and the Lord did not look for His glory in withdrawal into depths of unapproachable light, but in fulfilment of His redemptive work, seen no longer by men, but in full view of principalities and powers in heavenly places.

He departed, having obtained eternal redemption for us. He could depart in a different frame from that of His servants who leave the world. It seems a trivial, hardly a reverent comparison to compare Him with them, but it is worth making, in order to bring out the greatness of the contrast. We carry out our little schemes, found our Societies, pass our Acts of Parliament, or at *best*, influence for good the shifting transitory opinion of the day. *He* departed, having obtained eternal redemption for us, not a thing to be *superseded* by the lapse of ages, but to be worked out by and through the ages, to grow in significance as it *is* growing to-day. He left the world with all the misery in it, but He left something else.

This is a sufficient answer. But there are answers which, though sufficient, do not satisfy. They produce outward silence, but there is still a voice complaining in the heart. We shall do well to listen to it. We shall all the better realise our position.

"Here is One Who had virtue, wisdom, and influence enough to govern the world, even setting aside His Divine omnipotence, Who might have restrained a thousand evils, and changed unspeakably the course of history. According to the belief of His followers He had an immortal life, a body raised above the touch of suffering or death; and yet—He leaves the world.

46

"What might He not have done for His Church!

"Where would have been its scandals, its corruptions, its schisms, its persecutions, if He had remained with it to govern it Himself?

"What might He not have done for *me*! You say that everything depends on this season of probation. Why does He reserve the revelation of Himself till all is decided? One meeting face to face, and if He be indeed what you say He is, I could surrender at once.

"It seems to me that He went just when He had attained the power and the position which He wanted for His work. If He had been what you say He is, He would not have gone.

"I cannot hear those deliberate words 'I leave the world' with indifference or satisfaction, as you do. I cannot return to Jerusalem with great joy."

We must confess at once that there is an element of mystery in the answer. The value of freedom for the development of human character is clear enough. But it is accompanied by such risk and loss, that it appears to us fitting that the Divine scheme should minimise it. If man must have free will within, let there be at any rate every influence from without to guide and uphold him. But this is exactly what does not happen. Jesus leaves the world to remove from men the over-mastering influence of His presence in the flesh. The disciples had come to hang upon His lips. That was what their training had led to even before the Resurrection. But after the Resurrection, if He had permanently continued with them, their dependence would surely have been absolute.

Now plainly such a state, happy and safe as it would have been, would have checked development of character, would not have been adequate to the constitution of human nature, and those vast possibilities in it, which we barely guess at here. The sensible, visible presence of Jesus would have stunted the moral growth of His disciples. This may seem a hard, almost an irreverent thing to say. What could be better and happier for a man than to hang on the words of Jesus for every thought and act? It *will* be the best and happiest thing, but in the present life it would be premature.

However, even if this view commends itself to us, there is still an element of mystery in the answer. This withdrawal of the gracious compulsion of a visible Saviour might be safe for the first disciples. But what has been the result of it on the mass of believers, who have never seen Him at all? It is idle to speculate on what might have been, if every man had still the opportunity of meeting the Lord face to face in the flesh. I will not concern myself to answer such an inquiry. I will only point out that the Ascension of the Lord, being the Divine plan, seems to teach that the free development of human character is of such essential importance that it must be had at any risk.

Precisely the same difficulties face us, and precisely the same answer must be given when we consider the withdrawal of the Lord's visible presence from the Church and the world.

If the individual is left, at any rate a Church is provided for him, and that Church might look for visible, unmistakable guidance. Yet it is not so. His personal directions, so far as we know them, were scanty and, humanly speaking, unsystematic, and for lack of His visible guidance, so we are ready to say, the Church was split by schisms, darkened by corruptions, and made again and again the agent of persecution.

Here again the only explanation is that freedom of development was essential, and that freedom of development could not have been had if the Lord had sat in the midst of His Church as its visible Head, while it *could* be had if His guidance was given through the Holy Spirit. It needs strong faith in Him, and His dispensation, to believe that the final result will be worth the tremendous cost, but we do believe it.

And what we believe of the Church, we believe also of the world. This is harder still, even for an optimist. But we cannot think that Christ, leaving the world, was leaving it that it might grow worse and worse. The gloomy prospects of the later apostolic age must not be allowed to colour our views of the future. Something of good for the human race and perhaps for other spheres of existence is to be evolved here even apart from and outside the Church.

"I leave the world" is not a sentence of rejection.

This then is one side of the matter, one of the thoughts of this Ascension season, the necessary divinely ordained forsaking of the world, the Church, the individual, by One Who had apparently come to share permanently all the fortunes of man, a forsaking too at the very moment when He seemed qualified to carry out His great plan, and establish the Kingdom of God. "I leave the world", not merely the world in its limited hostile sense, but the world in the sense of human society, and the sphere in which it moves. This Jesus *leaves*.

But there is another side of the matter, an absolutely contradictory statement—"I am with you alway, even unto the end of the world". He is with His Church and with His people. He is with them by His Spirit.

This is our habitual view of the matter, at any rate *speculatively*. It is so much our habitual view, that it has perhaps been a perceptible effort to realise to-day the importance of the visible withdrawal of the Lord, and the questions which it raises as to the Divine intention in it.

We are, then, placed in a position which admits of two opposite descriptions, a world which Jesus has left, a world which He fills; a world which is set free to develop itself, a world which is in the closest dependence on Him spiritually as well as materially. It is not that these conflicting statements represent severally the opposing convictions of unbelievers and believers, but both are true. I bring them forward together not merely to arrange an antithesis, but to realise, if I can, the conditions under which my life is to be lived. The sense of the difficulty involved in Jesus leaving the world for which He might have done so much, quickens my assurance of His real invisible presence. I gain by having felt, by having complained of, by having been perplexed by, that almost cold, almost indifferent word of departure, "I leave the world".

Let us examine a little more closely this compatibility of independence and dependence, the possibility of realising both in our spiritual life.

My dependence on the Eternal Word for material needs is concealed with the highest art. The Reign of Law effectually prevents my feeling it, and is indeed an obstacle to my recognising it when I *desire* to do so, an obstacle which requires enlarged and lofty views of the Divine activity for me to surmount it. No interruption of those laws comes now to remind me that they are but the expression of His will, and the form of His force.

But my dependence on Him for spiritual guidance and support is, so far as I can see, on a different footing. I fear to limit the vast unknown work of the Holy Ghost. But it seems as if spiritual dependence on the Lord must be in great measure voluntary, a dependence of choice. He alone can adequately supply spiritual needs. In that sense all are dependent on Him *potentially*. But there is no *actual* dependence till the needs are awakened—till we seek to *have them supplied*. There *is* a state of actual spiritual dependence, but it is only reached gradually by effort and surrender. The work of life is the voluntary transformation of independence into dependence. That which is ignoble politically and socially is noble in the spiritual sphere and towards the Lord. It is the voluntariness of the surrender, the faith involved in it, the effort that it requires, as towards One Who is unseen, which make it the means of perfecting our nature. Our freedom is freedom to surrender. God made us free, the Ascension leaves us free, for *this*.

Let us examine the matter in actual experience. Here is one who is absolutely ignorant of Christ in everything, except in name. The Eternal Word fills all things, sustains the universe, but *he* sees nothing but the laws of His action. As to spiritual guidance, help and support, he has none of it, except in an indirect way. Worldly, or may I rather say cosmic motives and hopes, human friends cheer or fail him. For him Jesus has left the world. He is allowed to think so, if he chooses. Here is another whose whole soul rises up against such an assertion. The Lord is with him all the days. He sees His hand in every turn of his life. More than this, he is living a life of which Jesus is the motive and the support. He has come by Grace to be absolutely dependent on Him. He knows it is a precariously enjoyed dependence. He trembles lest he should lose it. But as it is, he is the bond-servant of Jesus Christ. How he rejoices when he feels the constraining power of His will, his inability to think or speak or act apart from Him!

Yet the commonest case lies between these two. A man feels the great presence near him at times, but his experience is one of alternating nearness and separation. He is still liable to fall back into the *illusion* of a life without God, a world without Christ. But even this experience bears testimony that Jesus is here.

This season, then, is the Festival of the Unseen. In it we assert against detractors the power of human nature to know and live by what no eye beholds. And not merely that human nature *can* do this, but that it is the way of its perfection.

For some no doubt this is a harder task than for others; so much so, that there are times when, in spite of our assertions of the universality of Christianity, it seems open to the old charge against the philosophies which it supplanted, the charge of being a religion for the *few*.

But the Gospel has more than one aspect. That is a profound truth with regard to it, capable of a hundred illustrations. Let us close with one of them. There is the retrospective view. Some minds are ever turning back to the past facts, the solemn, glorious, reassuring facts of the Lord's life. They live by these.

There is also the expectant aspect—waiting for the coming of the Lord Jesus Christ. The Christian watches, labours, occupies till His Master come.

Both these are looking on things which are not seen, and eternal.

But there is a third aspect which tries the spiritual sight still more, though lying nearer; yet perhaps when habitually attained it has more power to govern life. It is to see *now* and *here*, between the faces of the crowd, Jesus everywhere present, to feel, to live by His presence. This is no matter of the imagination, no property of an emotional nature. It comes by the plain matter-of-fact way of regular habits of devotion, and in no other way: O that we used them more! Those who attain it can understand the words which He spoke: "A little while and ye shall *not* see Me, and again a little while and ye shall *see* Me". They can follow Origen's splendid misinterpretation of St Paul, and say that *already* they walk not by faith but by sight.

VIII. WAITING FOR CHRIST

I. Cor. i. 7. *Waiting for the coming of our Lord Jesus Christ.*

We can all remember moments in our life when we waited for the coming of someone dear to us, some-one long divided from us by time and distance. The scene and place, the sounds and circumstances rise before the mind's eye, a crowded railway station or the quay of a seaport town. And this waiting may have been in very different frames of mind, in anxiety and suspense, in fear, or in joyful anticipation.

The *text* speaks of waiting for someone, but this waiting is different. It is not for a few minutes or an hour, but for a whole life. The life of the soul is a life of waiting. That is its pervading spirit, and runs through it all. We read *that*, everywhere in the Bible. Take the first expression of it which comes so strangely and suddenly in Jacob's blessing, "I have waited for Thy salvation, O Lord". Open the Psalter wherever you will, and waiting, hope, and expectation lie before you. Begin the New Testament with the Gospel of St Luke, you are at once in the midst of a circle of devout men and women whose characteristic is this—they are waiting for the consolation of Israel. Listen to Christ's own teaching. "Ye yourselves like unto men that wait for their lord." Go on to the Epistles, and hear how St Paul describes those to whom he writes. "Our citizenship is in heaven; from whence also we wait for a Saviour, the Lord Jesus Christ." The Christian life then is a life of waiting. How entirely out of harmony with the busy life of the present day is such a conception! That life comes on us morning by morning with its pressing duties, engrossing employments and amusements. Certainly it does not seem the right way to present Christianity to the men of to-day, to tell them it is a life of waiting. They will say, "I cannot wait; I have too much to do. Opportunities are passing at rapid speed". That is the feeling of the earnest, active man in regard to his worldly duties. And it is the same with us on the definitely religious side of life. Activity is what we are called to in the Lord's name. We are to redeem the time. We see the loss from the slow, pensive, waiting disposition which says "nothing can be done now, we must wait". And yet as we read the New Testament, waiting seems to overshadow the Christian life of the early Church. They were waiting for the coming of the Lord.

How can we reconcile these two conceptions of Christian life—untiring activity, engrossment in present duties, and a quiet spirit of expectation? It will be in some such way as this. In all our endeavours, in our inward and outward life we shall feel that completeness is not to be looked for, that everything here is of the nature of a beginning, whether for the individual or the Church or mankind. The Christian waiting is not waiting to act, but waiting for the result, for the effect, for the success, for the blessing. In many things there is little progress, for what is to come of them we must wait. So we turn to something else, and again to something else.

All work for the Kingdom of God is part of a great scheme, not a human scheme but a Divine purpose, not a purpose to be accomplished at once, or by one generation, but needing long ages to show what it is and whither it tends. A strong faith quickened by the Spirit of God gives us at times glimpses of that eternal purpose, the working out, under material conditions by beings endowed with free will, of moral values, purity, truth, justice, love, and all. It is some dim surmise of this Divine purpose which answers our question why God has made us as we are made and set us in the midst of temptation and pain. But the results are not attained here, the consequences of our trial are not made manifest, mysteries are not solved, problems are not settled. In many things all that is possible is effort, now in one direction, now in another. I do not speak to discourage effort. Yet it must be effort sobered, calmed, consoled in failure by the conviction that when most active, when every nerve is strained, we are still waiting, waiting for the coming of our Lord Jesus Christ.

"Waiting"; that word does not do justice to the Greek original. It is a special word with a connotation of eagerness and longing concentrated in one direction. In the New Testament it is almost always of the outlook of the believer to the return of the Lord.

There was a special pressure on the Church of the first days, the pressure of persecution. They were waiting for Christ to deliver them. There was no need then to urge this expectation as a needful element of Christian life. We see in the Epistles of St Paul and St Peter how large a place it held. Thank God that is not our experience to-day! The Church of Salonica was in danger of being too much absorbed in waiting for Christ. We are too little conscious of that great hope. Still we have reason enough to turn to it. How vain our efforts seem to be to stem the tide of intemperance, crime, and practical unbelief! How tangled and ravelled are the complications of our social life, how hopeless seem the questions at issue between capital and labour, secular and religious education, the treatment of criminals, the government of subject races, the marriage law! It is not enough to labour for truth and righteousness in these regions, we must labour and wait.

Take another thought. How the difficulties of faith increase upon us! Or rather I should say how adverse to faith is the habit of mind in the society of the day both high and low. How hard is the trial imposed on faith in revelation, which critical study imposes even on those who are preparing for the ministry of the Church! How evident are the divisions within the Christian fold, in the Church Universal and in our own Church! We are not to desist from effort. That is not the meaning of waiting for the Coming. We are to labour for unity with a large view of the freedom of the Gospel, and the variety of institutional religion which different races have a right to claim. Yet all the while we are to labour in the spirit of expectation. When the Head is manifested, then and not till then will the body be gathered into one.

We are waiting, but for what? I should rather say for Whom?

It is not merely for a Day of the Lord, for a great outburst of heavenly glory, for a revelation of the spiritual world, and a passing away of things which are temporal.

It is a *Person* for Whom we wait. Let us go back to those homely thoughts and private recollections with which we began. It is a Person, with human face and human heart, the Son of Man.

IX. THE SECRET THINGS OF GOD[1]

Deut. xxix. 29. *The secret things belong to the Lord our God, but the things that are revealed belong to us and to our children.*

These words are taken from the last of the great discourses in which Moses repeats the Law, and presses it home on the heart of Israel. In this third discourse he has set before them the certain consequence of disobedience—the extirpation of the race and the curse on the land. He has still some gracious words to speak of possible repentance and restoration. But at this point he pauses for a moment to remind them that their concern is with the present, not with speculation as to the future. In one aspect the future lies hid in

[1] Preached in Salisbury Cathedral, Sept. 8th, 1918.

the foreknowledge of God. In another aspect it is in their own hands. If the secret things belong to the Lord God, the things that are revealed belong to them and to their children, the words of the Law to keep them and to do them. Taken in this sense the text is an answer to every nation anxious as to its destiny.

Things revealed and withheld

But I want to expand the application of the passage and to give it a larger meaning. The present has its secrets as well as the future. The distinction between what God reveals and what He withholds is clearly drawn. I will not now dwell on what God has unveiled for us in the spiritual sphere, whether by His Son, His Spirit, or His Word, or by the individual experience of His Saints. The Bible is the history of revelation. But there are two regions which God has not unveiled—the world of departed spirits and the conditions and circumstances of life after the Resurrection. These are secrets of the Lord our God. But they are matters of supreme interest for ourselves, and therefore if any clear revelation in these respects is withheld, we may surely infer a definite Divine intention in their concealment. That is the point which I desire to insist on.

The World of Departed Spirits

Let me state the matter a little more fully. There is a veil which hangs between us and the world of departed spirits. How darkly that veil comes down when the last breath has been drawn! How impermeable it is! He was here a moment ago. Where is he now? All means of communication are gone. I know of course that there are many who say that they have found means of converse, and that the secret things beyond the veil are only waiting for scientific investigation. It is not my purpose now to inquire into the trustworthiness of the evidence alleged, or the further question of the legitimacy of such endeavours. It is enough to say that there is every appearance of an intention to conceal, of a veil divinely drawn between the living and the dead, totally different from the openness and freedom with which God has offered the secrets of the material world to the scientific inquirer.

Resurrection and Judgment

Then there is another secret closely connected with the first, but distinct from it—namely, the future life of the blessed, its circumstances and conditions after the Resurrection and after the Judgment. There is an endeavour to-day to set aside the expectation of a general resurrection and a final judgment, to treat both as elements of popular Jewish Apocalyptic employed by Christ, but not bearing the stamp of His authority, or at least not to be understood literally. We are asked to believe that the judgment upon our life here will be self-spoken, not divinely pronounced, and that it will come to each man separately. And instead of a general resurrection we are to expect that on our departure from the world each man is at once invested with the body that shall be. I only mention this teaching to say that I do not see how we can accept it if Scripture is the rule of faith. I would remind you of the words of the Creed—"He shall come again with glory to judge both the quick and the dead". There is an intermediate, disembodied state, and there is also a state beyond it after Resurrection and after Judgment. As to the conditions and circumstances of that state revelation is withheld, or at most imparted in terms which we recognise at once as symbolical.

Two Secrets which belong to God

Here, then, we have two definite Divine refusals to draw aside the veil; secret things which belong to the Lord our God. We cannot go beyond the solemn words of Heraclitus five hundred years before the coming of Christ. "There await men after death such things as they neither expect nor imagine." Yet we have before us at the present time within the Church a freely-expressed determination not to rest content with the absence of revelation in these respects. Is this a right attitude? That is the question. What I want to do to-day is not so much to challenge the method of discovery now proposed for either case as to suggest reasons why no revelation of the kind desired has been given us.

Converse with the Departed

We begin such an inquiry with sure confidence in the love and the wisdom of God, a confidence which comes of personal knowledge of Him. We are sure that all His dealings with us are in love and wisdom. We only ask that He would show us how His love and wisdom are manifest in what He withholds as well as in what He has revealed. First, we should perhaps expect that His love would repair the loss which comes by the separation of those whom His goodness has united here in bonds of tender affection and mutual reliance; that He would repair it by permitting some converse with the departed, some continuance of the help and guidance which has been taken away. The widow whose life has been lived in and with the life of her husband, the husband whose faith and obedience have been largely supported by the clearer faith and fuller obedience of the wife—is it needful that death should so absolutely separate them?

Wider Considerations

But in all questions concerning the providence of God we must remember that His providence has to deal with mankind at large and upon the whole, not only with the individual case and its bitter sorrow. The individual case personally known to us makes the strongest appeal to our emotions, but must nevertheless be viewed as one of countless instances, and we must ask what would be the effect on human life here as a whole if that converse which is so earnestly desired, became general. There is still a further question, which I do not want to raise, whether such converse would be good or even possible for those beyond the veil. There is room for doubt on both these points. Now let us try to conceive the complications which would result from influence and guidance reaching us here not merely from one or two of the departed, but from the vast world behind the veil. Imagine the effect first in family life and then again in the life of the nation. Cannot we see that such communications would frustrate the purpose of God that each individual and each generation should work out their own development in His strength and with His grace? We depend on one another to a degree that few realise, but it is a dependence limited in time, manner, and opportunity. Were these limits removed our independence would be paralysed. As it is, we still owe much to those who have left us, to their words, their very countenance and expression which dwell in our memory, their example, and their writings. All these remain with us as sources of strength and guidance. But personal converse is broken off for a time, and I think we can see why.

Special Dangers

This intercourse with the departed would tend to divert the soul from God. Reliance on such communications, if freely granted, would supersede that earnest longing for the guidance of the Holy Spirit which takes so large a place in the prayers of the believer. Those who have gone from us would take the place of God, not indeed as to worship, but as to much of that daily recourse for direction which now leads us to the Throne of Grace. I do not speak of the kind of answers which have hitherto been reported, for they are certainly not of the character of guidance. I am thinking of such messages of real significance as might be expected if the way were open for them.

Let me recall the indignant question of the most spiritual of the Old Testament prophets (I mean Isaiah) to the necromancers of his time. "Should not a people seek unto their God? On behalf of the living should they seek unto the dead?" And I may add that the transition from prayer for guidance to prayer for help is inevitable. Indeed it is already freely suggested that we owe defence and protection to our departed friends, that we are to recognise their action in the deliverance and inspirations of which we are conscious, and that they are God's instruments for our welfare. That God uses personal instruments for our welfare I do not doubt. But Scripture throughout shows us angels as our guardians, and not the spirits of the departed. The care of Beatrice for Dante's salvation does much to give the *Commedia* its indescribable charm. It is throughout the story of what one soul obtained for another by prayer and love. But it is to Scripture, not to mediaeval theology, that we must look for truth as to things unseen.

Life after the Resurrection

Let us pass on to consider the other secret. Much has been told us in general terms as to the blessedness of the Risen Life, but its conditions and circumstances are not revealed to us in distinct outline. At least one may say that the revelation is more negative than positive. There shall be no more death, nor sorrow, nor crying, neither shall there be any more pain. There are moments when this seems enough. We do not ask to know more. But in health and strength and consciousness of mental power these negative hopes are not sufficient. We want to know more, especially as to occupation, service, and progress. Why is the nature of that blessed life one of the secret things of the Lord God? Simply because its conditions and circumstances are not communicable in human language or as yet apprehensible by human faculties, both of which have been formed by experience here, and are incapable of going outside that experience; therefore they must be clothed in parables and symbols which appeal to the as yet undeveloped inner self, and which speak to the heart rather than to the reason.

The Value of Symbolism

Symbolism has its dangers. It is always in peril of being grossly and literally understood and dwelt on. Many popular hymns are to blame for this, and give occasion for the charge that Christianity offers nothing but a heaven of psalm singing. Interpret the symbolism, and we can see that the perpetual attitude of praise has a real significance. It is inseparable from the vision of God, in the depths of which vision heart and intellect alike will find satisfaction, infinite in experience, and so infinite in expression. That is what is meant by endless praise. It is the inevitable attitude of the soul. Does the symbolism of the final chapters of the Apocalypse need defence or apology? Is it said that it is poetry, and that we want fact? Do not such words show an ignorance of the very nature and function of poetry? True poetry is universal. It can reach and can interpret both the most refined and delicate mind and the simple emotions of the common man. Both can draw from the vision of the heavenly city assurances and comforts which cannot be put into words, which they welcome in the form in which God has given them, and find them enough. "Blessed are they that wash their robes, that they may have right to the tree of life and enter in by the gate into the city." "Blessed are they that are called to the marriage supper of the Lamb."

Our Interest in the Future Life

Now it is said that the prospect of a future life has very little hold on the minds of ordinary men, and that this is due to the want of clearer conception of it. It is said that symbols should be wholly laid aside, and a new view of the hereafter constructed from other sources. We have had examples given us in recent books. First, as to the slight hold which the future has upon our thoughts. It is not for the want of clearer views but from our natural constitution. The late Dr Mozley, in his sermon on Nature, has pointed out that Nature makes life an enclosure, and the reason is that it is essential that man should be able to. keep up his interest in the world and its affairs, and devote his attention to them. There is nothing amiss in this, it is God's purpose. Our clinging to life and the unwillingness of the Christian to depart, even when possessing the fullest hope of the life to come, are consequences of the Divine economy by which the thought of death is more or less excluded from our view. God meant us to live our life here and not to be diverted from its duties. So He bound the spirit to the flesh by most intimate ties, and kept from us any overwhelming view of the things beyond.

Prayer instead of Guesses and Inventions

If we need more light, the way to obtain it is not by guesses and inventions, but by prayer. In a recent book there is a passage by Miss Dougall on the characteristics of true and effectual prayer. It is a passage of value and beauty. It implies that by such prayer we may attain clearer views of the life hereafter. No Christian will dispute that. But I believe that the answer to such prayer will be not in the disclosure to the individual of secret things hitherto unrevealed, but in a deeper conviction of the wisdom and love of God, which will make all desires for detailed information sink to the level of mere curiosity. This I think is what the writer teaches us when she bids us seek to know more of "the Undiscovered Country".

What we do know

In conclusion, lest it should seem as if we knew nothing about that country, let us dwell on what we do know. First, there is something quite left out in the prospect as it is given us in the theology of the day. It is the joy of salvation—"I am saved". All doubt and fear at an end, and this poor unworthy soul finally and for ever delivered from sin and guilt. Call this egoism if you will, but the common joy of the redeemed is compacted of such egoisms. And they will merge at once in the joy of an innumerable multitude. Does the Psalmist say, "O visit me with Thy salvation"? Why does he ask for salvation? "That I may see the felicity of Thy chosen and rejoice with the gladness of Thy people and give thanks with Thine inheritance." Then there is the victory of Christ, the vindication of all that we have struggled and fought for in His Name. Here Christ's claims are scorned, His words set at naught, and His enemies prevail. There He will reign, and of His Kingdom there shall be no end. Then again there is the blessedness of entering upon the new spiritual body, and proving in the future all its mysterious capacities, the body of glory conformed to the likeness of the Risen Christ. This is "the hope of glory" of which we daily speak in the General Thanksgiving, the restored completeness of our whole personality which will for a time have been in abeyance. Some of you may remember the answer of the Saints in Paradise to the question of Beatrice, whether their joy will be greater after the Resurrection. "When our flesh has been put on again glorious and holy, our person will be more acceptable to God for being complete" (*Paradiso*, xiv. 43–66).

The Communion of Saints

Then there is the Communion of Saints of which as yet we have barely a foretaste. I need not dwell on the restoration of the close ties of affection broken for a time with so much anguish and reunited with so much joy. There is more than that. There is the entry into the vast fellowship of the servants of God in all

ages, and the effect on our souls of personal intercourse with them, an effect transcending our powers
of imagination. And this fellowship will afford infinite scope for the energy of love. If life has taught
us anything it has taught us that love is our supreme
happiness. Lastly, there is the vision of God, and in
that vision our affection and our intellect will find a
satisfaction which knows no end. "They shall be
satisfied with the plenteousness of Thy house; and
Thou shalt give them drink of Thy pleasures as out
of a river. For with Thee is the well of life; and in
Thy light shall we see light."

X. THE PRIESTHOOD OF CHRIST[1]

Heb. iv. 15. *For we have not an high priest which cannot
be touched with the feeling of our infirmities; but was in
all points tempted like as we are, yet without sin.*

The Epistle to the Hebrews tells us of the priesthood of Christ by which He reconciles man to God.
It shows us how that priesthood consists not only in
His power to reach God but in His power to reach
man.

Towards God He has a sacrifice to offer, the sacrifice
which the Father appointed, once offered for us all,
able to bring man in before God, pardoned, accepted,
beloved.

But the power of approaching God would be of no
avail, if He had not also the power of approaching

[1] Ordination, Trin., 1893.

man. Therefore Jesus has a human heart, and human sympathies, which attract and draw us to Him. He is felt to be One Who has experienced and overcome temptation. His human life and its character are known to us. He can be touched with the feeling of our infirmities. His goodness is the goodness which is formed and developed in conflict with evil. If on the one hand He can take us to God, on the other we feel that He can lay hold of us, that we are attracted to Him. It is the union of these two qualifications which makes Him our priest.

So far as the Christian ministry is a priesthood, that is to say a ministry for reconciling man to God, it must have the same twofold qualification as that higher ministry of Jesus, which it continues, and represents. It has a legitimated and assured access to the Divine mercy in Christ, a power of proclaiming it and assuring men of it. But this is nothing, unless it also has access to what is even more difficult of approach, the human heart in its infinite variety of disposition. What will give us that access? Not merely that we are fellow-men. Something more is wanted. We may learn what is wanted from our text, or rather from the example of Christ which the text sets before us. A life which is seen to be touched with feeling for human infirmities, which is subject to human temptations, which is, I will not say, without sin—no indeed —but in which those temptations are evidently overcome, in which falls and failures are turned to account for good, in which truth, purity, and love are being developed in and by the conflict with evil—it is such a life as this that will give us access to men's hearts for our priestly work, and will attract them to us. It is not merely a life in which there is temptation, as there is in their lives—for our liability to temptation they know well enough, even if we hide it—but a life in which temptation is not hidden, but seen to be overcome. In short, your personal moral life is as essential a qualification for the work of your priesthood being effectual as it is for your own individual accept-ance with God in Christ.

But before dwelling further on these thoughts, let us consider the Christian ministry in this aspect as reconciling and guiding men individually—and let us consider how far it is fulfilling this work in England to-day.

There is a need that you, my brethren, who are to-day called to the priesthood should do this work. It is wanted.

I do not, of course, mean that the soul of man cannot go direct to the throne of God without any human intervention or assistance whatever. I do not mean that the human conscience cannot receive from the direct guidance of the Spirit all that it needs to inform its judgments. That is so theoretically. But as a matter of fact, looking back at the spiritual history of human lives where they have been fully related to us, we see how much they have depended for the turns they took, on human priesthood, on the ministry of reconciliation, on the ministry of guidance. Men would be the better for much more of it than they ask

71

for or get at present, and that not merely the un-educated, but also the educated. A word of authoritative assurance of the love of God, what power it might have to set up again true and happy relations with the heavenly Father! A word of authoritative guidance on some plain moral duty, plain enough in itself, but hidden from the questioner by his own self-deceit, what power it might have to dispel delusion, how gladly and unhesitatingly it might at once be received and obeyed, calling out the obscured conviction and meeting the awakening conscience! These things are just what many lives are needing at the present moment in the parishes where you will be called to serve.

Such is the need of our day. Yet how little is being done for it. How little in many places the priesthood of the Church of England has to do with the inner lives of men. I say of *men* specially. Ask the clergyman of a parish how many men there are in his parish with whom he has had unreserved conversation, real *conversation* as to their spiritual needs. Those to whom he has given warning, comfort, instruction, may be many, but how many are there to whom he is in the happy relation of a trusted guide and counsellor as to the way of God? Ask yourselves this question two years hence when you are established in the charges on which you are now entering.

It is an acknowledged defect in our Church work. It is not only a public want, but one which you will personally feel. Men will not come and open their minds to you, even when you have got to know them, nor will you be able to reach them when you try.

What is the reason of this? Is it some deficiency in the methods of the English Church? Is it the absence of a definite and universally prescribed system of auricular confession? Is it therefore the duty of every newly ordained priest to co-operate openly or secretly with those who are labouring to re-establish that system? I have no wish to enter into controversy on that point, least of all on such a day as this, and am content to say that in my judgment this is *not* what is wanted, and that to work for it, is *not* your duty. The cause of the *in*efficiency of this ministry of individual reconciliation lies, I believe, in great measure in ourselves. The majority of Englishmen of to-day will not accept us simply for our office, will not come to receive formal guidance, and deem it sufficient, because it is authorised. It is not that they *disregard* authority or pay no regard to our special commission, but that they look for something more along with it. They will only seek and take guidance from persons of a certain character, I mean character in its moral sense.

If we could really hear what they are saying, I think it would prove in many cases to be something like this: "I cannot go to him, or send for him. He is a good man, I daresay; I have no fault to find with him. Only I feel that I could not open out to him, and that I should not get from him what I want". How widely this language is held, and with regard to how many conscientious and active clergy, it would perhaps surprise us to discover.

To what sort of a man will they go, to what sort of a man will they open themselves when he comes to them? To an eminently holy and devout man whose life is strongly marked off from the ordinary life of the world by its spirit of gentleness and heavenly-mindedness? No doubt such a character attracts many. Its very unlikeness to themselves would give it for them a charm and a power, to which they would gladly surrender themselves. But we cannot look for the development of such a character in the mass of our English clergy, even though it is their duty to aim at it. For this is not so much the result of special effort and grace, as the combination of these with special inborn endowments of disposition.

And on the whole I believe the mass of Englishmen would more naturally turn for guidance to one more like themselves, to one in whom their own conflict was more evidently going on. Show them a man who in every part of his daily life is fighting the good fight. They see him irritated yet patient, insulted yet full of forgiveness, with pleasure and amusement at his command yet tasting sparingly of it. They see him scrupulous in his avoidance of temptation and that not merely for propriety's sake but from a watchful sense of his own weakness; minutely careful in every particular of duty however disagreeable; truthful to a word in common conversation, and in matters where his pecuniary interests are affected; eager to cast out every jealous, envious, and suspicious thought the moment it arises; determined that nothing shall make him take offence; tenderly considerate of every human infirmity. They see all this going on not without an effort, but with efforts which draw their strength from some secret inward spring, which is really nothing less than union with Christ, and the constant renewing of the Holy Spirit.

Thus they see him tempted and overcoming. And when they see him *overcome*, they are attracted still *more*—the frankness with which he owns his fault; the distress and shame about something which otherwise they would have thought trifling, reminding one of Dante's Virgil:

> O clear conscience and upright,
> How doth a little failing wound thee sore!

the evident gain of resolution and meekness, which come to him by his fault; his simple humility, as before his superiors, towards those who know that they are ten times more guilty—all this makes men say, "Here is a real man, and here is real religion. He is like us, and yet there is something living and moving in him which is not in us. What is it? Let us learn from him. He can help us".

Your ministry may depend for its validity upon the gifts and commission which are sealed to you to-day. But you will depend, for your opportunity and power of *exercising* it, on the thoroughness of your own moral life.

That moral life must of course depend for its existence on the devotional life behind it. I might speak to you of that, I know it would be welcome, but I am anxious in these few words to keep to *one point*. Perhaps too there is less need to urge the devotional life. I do not doubt that you mean to cherish that inner life by every means, and that you already find in it a deep source of joy and strength. But it is the moral life, as outwardly manifested, which will put you in touch with those whom you have to reconcile and to guide.

It is the life *itself* which will do this, not the ability of talking about it. Preaching is a great power. The opportunity which preaching gives of speaking unreservedly not to one but to many, of shooting arrows at a venture, which you would have no right to aim at individuals—these and other facilities which it has, help the preacher to gain in public and beforehand that private access to men about which we are speaking. And it is well that you should bear in mind that aspect of preaching, as a *way to your people's confidence*. But preaching can do nothing without the life. If it does not have its counterpart there, it will destroy confidence instead of begetting it.

In thus earnestly pressing on you the need of a thoroughly consistent moral life in the little matters of daily intercourse as the condition of access to men's hearts for the greater things of your ministry, I am not bidding you aim at it for the sake of that, for the sake of influence. God forbid. That would be beginning from without instead of from within.

Only I would say, if you find your influence small, if you find shyness, uncommunicativeness, absence of really close spiritual relations with the men of your parish, ask yourself *why it is*. You may be popular, and in secular matters influential. You may have a following among the younger men in the recreative and educational side of your work. You may have a

following of older men in philanthropic and ecclesiastical matters, but yet it may be that you have not got
spiritual influence or spiritual access to either the one
or the other.

It is not because you are young, or because you are
reserved, or because there is a want of Church tone
in the parish. No, it is your own life which, notwithstanding your diligence in fixed duties, has not brought
home to them the conviction that they will find in
you real living religion, strong to combat the doubt
of the mind and the temptations of the flesh. Till this
conviction is born in them, no official claim to reconcile
and guide will be of any avail.

How was it with the Lord Himself? Did He begin
His ministry by enforcing His claim as the Son of
God, and the Mediator between God and man? No,
He let His life and character work. These gave Him
access to men's hearts, and opportunity for His
healing, reconciling, guiding work. They saw Him
touched with the feeling of their infirmities, tempted
like as they were, yet without sin.

It will be with you in your measure, as it was with
Him. Can you ask for a better way than His? Your
temptations, your victories, your falls, your peni-
tences, your personal sorrows and disappointments,—
all these will give material which will manifest your
character, or rather, manifest the power of Christ in
you—all these will draw and attract men to you, will
give you access to their hearts. It will never be said
of you, "I cannot go to *him*, I cannot speak to *him*".
There may be those who will shun you because they

wish to hide the evil treasure of their hearts, but none will turn from you whom the Spirit of God has touched with the beginnings of awakening. With what joy you will feel that, neither on the side of God nor on the side of man, is there anything to hinder the exercise of the highest function of your Christian priesthood.

"Now then we are ambassadors for Christ, as though God did beseech you by us: we pray you in Christ's stead, be ye reconciled to God."

XI. LOVE OF THE UNSEEN CHRIST[1]

I. Pet. i. 8. *Whom having not seen, ye love.*

Our Saviour when He came to visit us in great humility was not content with reverence, obedience, belief. He desired love, the *love* of His disciples, and it was given Him.

He desired it for His *own sake*, as perfect man. He would not have been perfect man if He had not desired to be loved. But He desired it also for the sake of His disciples. He desired that they should *know* Him; and knowledge depends upon love, just as truly as, in another aspect, love depends on knowledge. He desired that they should obey Him from the *heart*, and that is the obedience of love.

So He desired to be *loved* by them, and the love came. What is the picture which we have in the Gospels? An outside crowd receiving blessings, lis-

[1] Preached in the Chapel Royal, St James, Nov. 30th, 1919.

78

tening, admiring, welcoming, questioning, and at last forsaking. And an inner circle gradually drawing nearer and encircling Him with personal love.

But when He was gone, and the Apostles were left with the task of drawing others in, of gathering them round the now Unseen Christ, was this love to Him to be asked for from *them*, to be required in those who formed the new Christian community? Was that love even *possible* for those who had not seen Him? Surely they were in a different position. Love comes by sight and intercourse. Ever so little is sometimes enough, but *that little* is indispensable. True it is that we often speak of love of characters in past history, or of contemporaries never yet seen by us. But then we mean a different thing. It is only by a considerable extension of the word that we can say we love such a man as Alfred the Great or such a woman as Joan of Arc. It is their memory which enchants and touches us.

What I speak of now is love to a person within our reach. This love the Apostles themselves still felt to the Living Christ, Whom they had seen and heard and touched, Whose face and expression and tones of voice and manner and movement were ever in their mind's eye.

Could this love be looked for at all in those who had believed by their word? Must they not be content to awaken in *them* reverence, belief, obedience, but not personal love?

They thought otherwise, and they found it otherwise.

Here in the text is what St Peter found. Translate the words precisely, and it runs thus: "Whom (though ye never saw Him) ye love". And St Paul at the close of his great Epistle to the Churches of Asia includes them all in one description: "Grace be to all them that love our Lord Jesus Christ in sincerity".

St Paul's *own* love to the Saviour, seen but once with his bodily eyes on the road to Damascus, nevertheless occupied his heart and life, and was the *constraining power* of his ministry. He looked for it in others, he implanted it in those who heard him. It was with them, as with him, a personal affection to a living Master with Whom they had constant intercourse.

And this has been the relation of Christ's people to Him ever since. They have endured, laboured and lived in the love of Christ. Christianity has never been, at least in its true types, a mercenary religion, as its enemies have striven to represent it. It has been a religion of love, a service of love. And it is therein that it is superior to all other religions which men compare with it. It gets hold of what is best and strongest in man, namely love. That is the secret of its vitality. Where that is not its type, it is a fluctuating, uncertain thing, the sport of any wind.

Your Christianity is a religion of love, though strengthened and supported by devotion to duty, fixed habits, and the fellowship of the Church. You live consciously in the presence of an Unseen Lord, you address Him in prayer and praise, you partake of Him in His Sacrament, you offer Him your self-denials, your victories over temptation, your labours for your fellow-men. You turn to Him with confidence in the difficulties of life. You follow holiness, without which no man shall see the Lord. On this Advent Sunday you look forward, through death and whatever else may intervene, to His coming again in glorious majesty.

This then is our relation to the Saviour, not merely belief, trust, commitment, but personal affection. You desire to see His face.

This love must vary in force according to temperament. There is a mystic temperament for which the relation to Christ is as close as, or even closer than, any human friendship. Such hearts have experience of conversation with Christ. The book of Thomas à Kempis entitled *Of inward consolation*[1] is the record of such a colloquy, and we also know by our own experience that the voice of affection is heard and answered by Him to Whom it is addressed. We have conversed with Him.

But there is also a not less distinctly non-mystical temperament. None the less in its own way it is devout, simple, and true. The point for us all, whatever our temperament may be, is firmly to realise that daily and hourly we have to do with a *living* and loving Christ, Who asks for our love, our poor faint human love. Let no one be satisfied with anything short of giving Him *that*. It is not beyond our powers. What progress can we make in this matter, for with some there may perhaps be a real need of advance? On the one hand there are many to whom personal love to a living Saviour is *already* a main factor in

[1] I.e. Bk. III of the *De Imitatione Christi*.

their lives. They have cherished it by habits of discipline and devotion, and need no word of exhortation. For them the Advent prospect is this, that they will see face to face Him Whom they have long known, for, in the words of Eliphaz in the Book of Job, they have acquainted themselves with God, and *are at peace*. But we must not forget that there are many with whom it is otherwise. Shall we first seek to love Him more, and then to obey and serve Him more, or shall we begin with more thorough service and obedience and wait for love to grow? That was the Apostles' way, and it will be our best way also. It was not at the beginning, but at the *end* of the discipleship that the Lord asked Simon, "Lovest thou Me?" Love will grow by service and obedience, by confession of His name in a contemptuous world, by sacrifices and endurance for His sake, by His acceptance of them, by our *consciousness* of His acceptance. And moreover our love will grow along with our *increasing power* of perceiving and delighting in His moral beauty, in the dignity, tenderness, and wisdom of the one perfect human character, as we behold His glory full of grace and truth.

We must not anticipate or hurry this gradual growth. We must not make demands on ourselves, or let others make them on us, which we are not ripe to meet. That is why not a few of our hymns in common use are dangerous to religion. They put into the lips of a mixed congregation sentiments of intense affection, which, while they are for some most true and touching, are for others utterly unreal. And remember that love is not all of one kind. It has many forms, and therefore many modes of expression. There is a love which is above all things loyalty and adoration—which shrinks from familiarity and too near approach to the accents of common human fondness. This also is love.

There is another point on which a caution is needed. Much is said in books of devotion about complete concentration of the affections upon Christ, as though the existence of any other strong affection would interfere with our love to *Him*. That idea is a blemish in that wonderful book to which I referred just now, the book of Thomas à Kempis, *Of the Imitation of Christ*. St John writes very differently, and surely it is St John whom we may trust above anyone else in what relates to personal affection to our Lord. I need not quote, but only remind you that the whole tenor of his first Epistle is this, that love to God and love to man flow side by side from the human heart, and cannot in their fulness exist separately. Human affections are not a scanty exhaustible source, all of which must be reserved for Christ, a fixed quantity so to speak. No; they are large, elastic, illimitable. As they are drawn out to Christ they become fuller and deeper towards man, and may we not add towards nature, which is the work of God's hands. It is only when we recognise that other loves distract and pre-occupy us that we need fear them. So far as they are true and pure affections there can be no competition or collision with the love of Christ.

In conclusion let us go back to the text, "Whom

having not seen, ye love". There is a saying of St Paul
which we may put by the side of the saying of St Peter.
It is this: "We walk by faith, not by sight". The two
utterances are not synonymous. To *love* the Unseen
One is something more than to walk by *faith* in Him.
But they both present in different aspects that great
trial of human nature which is part of the Divine
purpose, the discipline by which the capacities of man
are to be strained to the uttermost for the realisation
of the *highest moral values*, and to be fitted thereby for
the employments of the life to come. At one moment
we are ready to say that love of the Unseen Lord
makes a demand upon us which we cannot meet, at
another the Cross rises before our eyes, and that
inward vision is enough for us. He knows the weakness and blindness of our spiritual sight. He reveals
Himself within us.

Yet even so, we hear from pure and humble souls the
same lament which Cowper has put into words for them:

> Lord, it is my chief complaint
> That my love is weak and faint.

I would answer, "Do we really know *ourselves*?
I think not". This coldness is but superficial. Let
someone whom you love name the name of Christ in
serious earnest at a thoughtful moment, and the response comes, there is the glow of heart within, there
is emotion in those four words—"per Iesum Christum
dominum". The Saviour knows us better than we
know ourselves. So we say like St Peter: "Domine,
tu nosti omnia: scis quia amo te. Lord, Thou knowest
all things; Thou knowest that I love Thee".

XII. THE PURPOSE OF GOD[1]

I. Sam. xvi. 11. *And Samuel said unto Jesse, Are here all thy children? And he said, There remaineth yet the youngest, and, behold, he keepeth the sheep.*

Let our imagination carry us back 3000 years. Let us stand at the gate of the little town of Bethlehem and look round us to see who are there. Here are the elders of the city anxious and trembling; in front of them Jesse and his seven tall sons, their faces dark with displeasure. High in the midst of them sits the aged prophet Samuel, the greatest man in the land, and all eyes are fixed on him in expectation. Then suddenly a lad breathless with haste enters the gate and stands surprised. He has been sent for, but why? He is ruddy and of a fair countenance, and goodly to look upon. The prophet arises and pours on the boy's head the sacred oil of kingship. Then the strange, incredible truth dawns on the boy. The purpose of God forces itself on his troubled mind and reveals itself in his face. Nor is this all. The Spirit of the Lord comes upon him mightily and with it the courage to receive and understand the new and amazing event. The crown and the throne are as yet far away. Many a conflict and years of exile and suffering lie between him and them. But the gifts and calling of God are irreversible, and the time will come when, in that magnificent eighteenth Psalm, David the servant of the

[1] Preached in the Lower Chapel of Eton College, Nov. 16th, 1916.

Lord will recall at the end of his life all his dangers and deliverances.

The Bible sets before us great types of critical human experiences which on a lesser scale belong to men in all times. Such is the case with this story. Something of the same convictions, some similar sense of a Divine purpose, of a work to be done, of an ambition which is not selfish, come to the young in unexpected moments. Until lately such convictions came but rarely. In former days there was little to disturb the careless, untroubled boyish life of daily pleasures and interests, and the prospect of the same or greater pleasures to come. Now things are changed. The seriousness of life makes itself felt, yes, and the possible shortness of life instead of that interminable vista of years which used to lie before us in boyhood. One great gain has been the banishing of low ideas of what boys want to do and to be. I do not think that any one of you would be satisfied to say or to feel that all he looked forward to in life was mere personal distinction and success for himself, even if it were distinction not in lower matters, such as sport and fashion, but in the nobler fields of professional or political life. Nothing like the anointing of David has come to you or is likely to come. But the conviction which fell on David that day, of God's strange and gracious purposes for him, does repeat itself in varying ways in the mind of many a lad. Life is not always going to be the perfectly and delightfully careless thing that it now is. You know that quite well. David was not always to keep the sheep, though even

THE PURPOSE OF GOD

in keeping the sheep he was to prove his courage against the lion and the bear. The lion and the bear are upon you now in the temptations of youth, and you have to master them as David did if you are to do greater things hereafter.

I do not want to encourage reveries or day-dreams as to the future. Live your happy school life fully, gladly, blamelessly. But it will be well if there be a purpose at the back of your mind, not perhaps of a definite time of action, but a purpose to serve God and your country in such ways as He shall show you. Will you be able to do this? Have you the gifts and powers? Perhaps you think you have not. It is good to undervalue yourself. But the fact is that the school registers which lie before us record services and attainments on the part of many of whom their schoolfellows expected little. It was said to me the other day of one of the most distinguished men of our time that at Eton they never found him out.[1] It is well that a boy should be diffident and modest, and should feel his weakness and inexperience when the prospect of responsibility and power first dawn on him, not very far away. You have listened this morning to the stirring record (Heb. xi) of the heroes of one particular nation, their triumphs and their sufferings. What inspired them? How did they endure and over-come? It was by faith, faith in God Who called them, Who guided and upheld them. How are they de-scribed? "Who through faith subdued kingdoms, wrought righteousness, obtained promises, out of

[1] Arthur Balfour.

weakness were made strong, waxed valiant in fight, turned to flight the armies of the aliens." What is Faith? It is one of those large words which we are too content to understand vaguely. But you know what trust is, what reliance means. You trust your friend, you depend on him. He is true, good, and strong. So you trust God. And what a friend! It is faith in God enthroned in majesty above the world, its maker and sustainer, faith in His righteousness and justice, His personal care for all His children, faith in His love manifested on the Cross on Calvary, in the Blood which atones for all sin. This is the faith which is sustaining England to-day, not present indeed in all who bear the English name, but in that sound, true kernel of English men and women who make the nation what it is.

And this faith in God's wisdom, love, and power will sustain you in your lives, and enable you to do and suffer things which you do not dream of yet.

Lastly, let us go back to David. "The Spirit of the Lord came mightily upon David from that day forward." The gift of the Spirit is the central thought of the Service of Confirmation. Some of you are shortly to be confirmed. I do not say that you, like David, will feel a sudden access of spiritual life and power—but what you expect, *that* you will receive. Ask in faith, nothing wavering. Ask for the Spirit of God to raise your desires, to awaken *new* desires unfelt before, to open your sight to things invisible and eternal, to confirm your resolutions, to inspire and remould those purposes of which I have been speaking. Ask for the

Spirit to remind you of those higher purposes when life is so full of happiness that you forget them. Ask Him to recall them to you when you have fallen into sin, and are tempted to think that they have passed away from you and can be yours no longer.

LECTURES

I. THE LITANY[1]

LECTURE I

In order to justify my choice of subject, I have only to say that the Litany is the service in which the congregation especially takes part and that its tone and character are in harmony with the season of Lent.

My examination of it will not be critical but devotional. I have indeed no claim to special liturgical knowledge. However, to-day I must say a little by way of introduction. After to-day I shall only examine the Litany critically so far as is necessary for purpose of interpretation. And here observe the difficulty of interpretation. We are not dealing with a homogeneous document. The Litany is like an ancient building built of much more ancient material, of which the stones are of all sorts of dates, formerly applied to quite different purposes. There are almost always two questions: (1) What is the original of such and such a phrase? and (2) What is its present sense in its present position?

This is true of all our services, and particularly of the Litany.

It is rather startling to find that the original place of the Litany was in the Liturgy. It represents those

[1] Salisbury Cathedral, Lent, 1896.

common prayers for all men which Justin Martyr mentions in that precious account which he has left us. It stands in the Eastern Liturgies, both in their earliest forms and to-day. It is also to a certain extent and for a certain period present in the Western Liturgies. This was recognised by the Reformers, and in the First Prayer Book of Edward VI the Litany follows immediately after the Order for Holy Communion. The use of the Litany in processions, which is so prominent in most accounts of the service, was only a special use, and should not be stated as the origin of Litanies.

Being used in the West in these processions for the purpose of averting calamity, it was specially open to a particular kind of corruption. It became the part of the service in which the Invocation of Saints was prominent. This increased, as time went on, to a very great extent. In the Sarum Litany there were twenty-eight Invocations for regular use and forty more for each day of the week.

Our present Litany, which came out in 1544, and was the first step in the revision of the ancient English services after the publication of the English Bible, is the earliest part of the Book of Common Prayer. There was a still earlier English Litany, but this was the first one which appeared with authority. We owe it to Archbishop Cranmer.

Comparing it with the Litany in the Sarum Processional we find several points of difference.

(1) It is much fuller; many of its most beautiful petitions have nothing corresponding to them in the Sarum book.

(2) The Invocation of Saints is omitted. In its first form (1544) the intermediate step had been taken of reducing the Invocations to three, but even these were left out in the First Prayer Book of 1549.

(3) It presents a definite method and order which were very much to seek in the Sarum Use. Nothing is so characteristic of the present Litany as its method and arrangement, of which I shall say more hereafter.

Whether we regard the devotional tone of the petitions or the masterly English in which they are expressed, our deep thanks are due to Almighty God for this work of Archbishop Cranmer.

Now after these words of introduction let us turn to the Litany itself.

The Invocations. All Christian prayer must begin by addressing Him to Whom we make appeal. The human analogy helps here; you make appeal to a friend by name. In the Old Testament to call on the Name of the LORD is to pray to Him. So the Litany begins with Invocations. They are the expansion of the *Kyrie Eleison* of the old services. These are so framed as to be a confession of the doctrine of the Trinity. The Godhead of each Person is acknowledged. But wherever the Godhead of each of the Three Persons is stated, we need the complementary thought of the One God; and so we have it here.

Observe that God the Son is called the Redeemer of the world. *Redemptor mundi* is not Biblical. *Salvator mundi* occurs once or twice, in John iv. 42, in I. John iv. 14, and in Gen. xli. 45 as the translation of Joseph's

Egyptian name in the Vulgate. But *Redemptor* means something more than *Salvator*. It recalls the cost; it anticipates what comes below in the Litany when we say, "Whom Thou hast redeemed with Thy most precious blood". And notice the relation of the blessing with which the Litany closes to the Invocations with which it begins. As in the beginning we call on Him for mercy, so we close with the assurance of that mercy in its threefold form. It is more than mercy or pity; it is the "Grace of our Lord Jesus Christ, and the Love of God, and the Fellowship of the Holy Ghost".

The Responses. "Have mercy" at first sight gives the idea of asking to spare. But *Miserere* with its Hebrew and Greek antecedents means "have pity". It is asking Divine compassion. Pity is not the same as mercy, nor quite the same as compassion. It is compassion in action. A man about to be punished cries, "have mercy"; a man long under suffering says, "have pity". Compare the Eleeson of blind Bartimaeus and other similar appeals in the Gospels. This gives the key to the meaning of "miserable". Fault is often found with its use here as being unreal. And you are not, it is argued, miserable in the sense of *infelix*. But you are pitiable. We men are such as to call forth Divine compassion. O yes, and more than we know! "Pity us poor sinners" would be a clearer expression. Let us take it in this sense. Then the greatness, glory, and holiness of God will only add to the boon of His pity. It brings out the contrast. See above on the relation of the Grace to the Invocation.

And here in the early Litanies after the Invocation of God stood the Invocation of the Blessed Virgin, angels and saints. Let us endeavour to treat this fairly and take it at its best, not as in the practice of the Roman Church to-day, a very different thing, but following the lead of Bellarmine, the greatest of Roman controversialists.

It rested on another doctrine, viz. that certain holy persons instead of being in the intermediate state were, because of their holiness, in the immediate presence of God. This of course has to be proved. But, supposing them to be in this special position, for which I think there is no scriptural evidence, we may, it is argued, ask God to put it into the heart of the saints to pray for us, for they see all things in God, or at least all *quae pertinent*, and thus are aware of the invocations addressed to them by the living.

In consequence of these invocations they intercede for us with God; but this they, as well as all living beings do, *per Christum*. They are not independent mediators. So the unique mediation of Christ is *supposed* to be safeguarded. How far this is from being the case we may see from practice in Roman Catholic countries.

In answer to our argument that such intercession is unnecessary it is said: "Why then ask for the prayers of the living? If you ask for them, *a fortiori* you may ask for those of the same persons when dead". In reply I must be brief. We find no warrant in the New Testament. The prayers of the saints in the Book of Revelation (viii. 3) are clearly the prayers of living saints, presented, it is true, by angels; but this is a purely ministerial action, and does not justify our addressing them directly.

The conflicting passages from Church authors at a time when many corruptions had begun do not convince us to-day. The thing is not to be argued on such methods.

Secondly we see what it leads to in practice: the altars of the Virgin, and of saints in continental churches, and worshippers drawn away from simple approach to God. A belief which leads to such action as that is so perilous that we cannot accept it unless upon clear distinct evidence, evidence which in this case is not forthcoming.

The Deprecations, which are addressed to the Lord Jesus, as is clear from what follows.

We at once begin to see how methodical the present Litany is as compared with the Sarum Use.

First we ask for forbearance in exacting punishment. "Spare us" naturally precedes "Deliver us"; and the order marks a rising confidence in request.

Then we ask for deliverance from evil—*Libera nos a malo*—classified under two heads (*a*) Sin (in two verses), (*b*) Divine judgments (in three verses).

Taking these Deprecations in detail—why does the prayer for forbearance come first? It is the order of a scriptural litany, that of Joel ii. 17: "Let the priests, the ministers of the LORD, weep between the porch and the altar, and let them say, Spare Thy people, O LORD", etc.

The prayer itself is a recollection of various texts

of Scripture, its nearest parallel being a passage in the prayer of Tobit (Tob. iii. 3): "Remember me, and look on me, punish me not for my sins and my ignorances and the sins of my fathers, which sinned before thee".

And here there are two points to notice.

(*a*) "The offences of our forefathers." Is there any need to ask that *they* should not be remembered? Does not Ezek. xviii. 4, with its proclamation of individual responsibility: "the soul that sinneth, it shall die", put them out of account? That is true, but yet we do stand in a close relation to our forefathers. We do suffer for their sinning. This is represented as an intentional Divine dispensation in the Second Commandment, "visiting the sins of the fathers upon the children", and to go deeper and further back, it is implied as a principle in scriptural teaching as to the sin of Adam and its consequences. So while holding strongly to personal responsibility we may well pray to be relieved from the effects of inherited punishments. I own that this explanation is not quite satisfactory, and I doubt if there is any quite satisfactory explanation.

(*b*) "Redeemed with Thy most precious blood." This is fetched from I. Pet. i. 18, 19, "Knowing that ye were redeemed, not with corruptible things... but with precious blood... *even the blood* of Christ".

Try and enter into this ground of petition. It is like the words of the *Dies Irae*:

> Quaerens me
> Redemisti
> Ne sit labor ille cassus.

Ne sit labor ille cassus may be pleaded with God as well as with man.

Now turn to the first of the three verses which enlarge the clause which we have been considering. Compare the enlargement of the same phrase in the Catechism: "that He will keep us from all sin and wickedness, and from our ghostly enemy, and from everlasting death".

Notice that we ask first for deliverance from sin, then from the natural consequence of sin, i.e. wrath and damnation. That is the Divine order. And also notice the recognition of whence sin comes. The reality of a ghostly enemy is very strongly taught in the Litany. We must not smooth away what is so clearly taught. It may be, I will say it *is*, impossible to imagine adequately the existence of a personality which is absolutely evil. All attempts to represent it have failed, Milton's most of all. In such difficulty we must simply receive the Divine teaching as παιδεία. There *is* a personal, supernatural, absolute Evil, who works by craft and by might. We are exposed to him, open to his attack; and how little we think about it! But there is One who can protect us if we desire to be protected. "From the crafts and assaults of the devil, Good Lord, deliver us. *Libera nos a malo*."

LECTURE II

We pass to five prayers in which the *Libera nos a malo* is expanded. To Whom are they addressed? They come between "Remember not, Lord, our offences" and "By the mystery of Thy holy Incarnation"; so it is clear that they are addressed to the Lord Jesus. And if so, so also are the Obsecrations, "We beseech Thee to hear us, good Lord". For look to the end: "Son of God: we beseech Thee to hear us", "O Lamb of God...grant us Thy peace...have mercy upon us".

This direct appeal in prayer to the Son is rare in our service. There are one or two collects, and there is the latter half of the *Te Deum*, but these are exceptional. And our Lord's own teaching in the New Testament is to address prayer to the Father, "After this manner pray ye, Our Father...". A careful consideration of the Gospels, especially the Fourth Gospel, brings this out. In the Acts and Epistles there is indeed prayer to the Lord Jesus, but there again it is the exception, not the rule.

How then are we to justify this feature of the Litany?

(1) The exceptions, though few, are tolerably clear. The most commonly quoted is the prayer of St Stephen: Κύριε Ἰησοῦ, δέξαι τὸ πνεῦμά μου. And the exceptions give us guidance. It is for us, as it was for St Paul, in work for Him that we ask His aid, work for Him and His Kingdom.

(2) As we draw near to God through Christ, we find God in Christ: "I am in the Father, and the Father in Me". We are not to endeavour to *discriminate*. God is revealed to us in Christ. The Godhead in the Three Persons is the same. A disposition (and there is this disposition) to address all devotions to the Divine

Son because we can ascribe to Him human affections much as in ourselves is, I think, dangerous. The fact of the Litany being originally addressed to the Son does not oblige us all through to discriminate. Let us take the guidance given by the Invocations; it is needed in order to prevent the Litany from becoming a Litany of Jesus.

Now let us look closer at the Deprecations which, as has already been said, comprise one prayer for general deliverance *(Universario a malo libera nos)*, two prayers for deliverance from sin, and two for deliverance from punishment.

In this general Deprecation which is presently sub-divided, notice the order, the true order. First sin, and then punishment. It is on deliverance from sin that the Christian is to fix his eyes. "Thou shalt call His Name Jesus: for He shall save His people from their sins."

It may be necessary to emphasise deliverance from punishment in order to appeal to the hardened, carnal, unspiritual imagination. But at best that is an imperfect method. The true evil is sin. Sin carries punishment in it and comprises it. There can be no forgiveness of the sinful while they keep their sin. *Libera nos ab ira* would be a fatal prayer apart from *Libera nos a peccato*. Even Plato in the *Gorgias* knows enough to tell us that. It is the concentrating of the mind upon *Libera nos a damnatione* which is the fault of the Salvation Army.

And here let me offer a practical suggestion. The utterance of the prayer is not enough of itself. We know how utterly unavailing the cry *Libera nos a peccato* is without our own effort. A man might spend his life in saying the prayer and receive no answer.

To return. In other prayers sin is regarded as a chain and a band; thought is concentrated on the power of habit in respect of sin, depending in some way on our material constitution, on the relation of soul to body, so that each sin is not an independent act but a continuous thing. But besides this there is here another aspect of sin. It is partly from without. Four times the existence of supernatural evil is emphatically recognised in the Litany, four times the prayer is offered for protection against its activity; twice in these Deprecations, "from the crafts and assaults of the devil", "from all the deceits of the world, the flesh, and the devil", and twice again later, "beat down Satan under our feet", and "the craft and subtilty of the devil". You know that it has been thought that this is the primary sense of the petitions in the Lord's Prayer ῥῦσαι ἡμᾶς ἀπὸ τοῦ πονηροῦ; and the explanation of it in the Catechism recognises it as a part of the sense: "that He will keep us from all sin and wickedness, and from our ghostly enemy". And there is the strongly personal activity of the Tempter in the New Testament.

For some of us this is difficult to realise. Our mind refuses a Being absolutely evil and simply malicious. Again, we feel our own corruption, and that seems to account for all sufficiently. Again, we feel a natural reaction against mediaeval superstition and belief in multiplied and universal appearances of evil spirits. But let us submit. The sense of the mystery of our being, of our ignorance, comes in to help. We accept the teaching as παιδεία. As the good impulses which arise in us unbidden are in our belief a super-natural help; so the evil thoughts which arise in us unbidden are a supernatural attack, and to many it is a comfort to think that these are from without—ἔξωθεν. Our soul is the battlefield between Good and Evil.

Anyway here is a great danger from Satan depre-cated. And the danger is twofold. There are the crafts and the assaults.

I suppose that for most of us it is the *crafts* we fear; apparently unimportant negligences, blinding us to the sinfulness of the means employed, leading us to actions which have the guise of religion. So Satan has led Christian men into religious persecution of other Christian men, making them think they were doing it for Christ's sake. The *assaults* are when he employs sudden passions.

Peccata spiritualia. The Deprecations as to sin are divided into two. There are first the so-called spiritual sins, which differ from the others according to the old classification by not being in immediate relation to the senses. And there are the *peccata carnalia* which are in such relation—gluttony, sloth, avarice, unchastity. The *peccata spiritualia* come first because according to the scholastic philosophers they are the more heinous, being subject to less natural temptation. At the head of them Cranmer put *caecitas cordis*. It had come later in the Sarum Litany, but he put it first because it is *blindness* which prevents our *knowing* these sins. A knowledge of the truth about ourselves and about God is the first step in winning salvation. Surely we feel the need of this.

Then pride, which is the next bar to salvation. It is not only ignorance which baulks us, but self-satisfaction, self-dependence, independence of God and of man.

I must not dwell upon each of these sins. I will just pause for a moment at the phrase "all uncharitableness", i.e. all lack or defect of love in our dealings with others.

It is to be interpreted by Rom. xiv. 15, "Now walkest thou not charitably". What is meant is not merely a manifestation of what is inspired in some degree or other by envy, hatred and the like. Uncharitableness means all lack of love in our dealings with others. This helps us to understand how it is that humble, pure, devout souls are in danger of the sin of uncharitableness. Need So and So (we think of some pure hearts) pray to be delivered from uncharitableness? Yes, for they are lacking in active love and hence have in them the beginnings of envy and hypocrisy.

Peccata carnalia. These are enumerated in the Second Deprecation as to Sin. "Deadly sin" they are called. The term is not to be taken as referring to unchastity alone; the spiritual sins of the preceding supplication are all regarded as deadly. The expression occurs again in Article xvi: "Not every deadly sin..."

is unpardonable". It is a survival of the Roman distinction which the usage of the English Church has long discarded, though there are now attempts to revive it. On the foundation of one passage (I. John v. 16), ἔστιν ἁμαρτία πρὸς θάνατον, men built up a legal system dividing sins into mortal and venial, and then proceeded to differentiate the methods of dealing with them, and of exacting satisfaction for mortal sin.

Let us hear Origen on the passage of St John. "There are some sins to loss and some to destruction. What kinds of sins however are sins to death and what not to death but to loss, cannot I think be easily determined by any man."

To return to St John himself: what he says is that there is sin (not of one kind but of many) which separates from Christ and so from κοινωνία. This is πρὸς θάνατον. It is not a particular kind of offence that is punished with damnation, but it tends to result in a fall from grace. The very same sin may have this result in one case and not in another.

The fact is that all classification of sins is dangerous. The Reformers were accused of making all sins equal. But we may reject formal distinctions without doing that. Let us fix our minds on the word "deadly" and think, not of special kinds of sin, but on all sin in its stronger manifestations, when it is increasingly wilful and habitual, as tending to death.

Sin through deceit. Lastly there is another aspect of sin, as a deceit. We all desire good—that is what moves us. The world, the flesh, and the devil present false goods. We are to be prepared as we enter upon the world to find that often—not always, but often—what attracts us is really evil under an appearance of good. The Apostle in the Epistle to the Hebrews speaks of "the deceitfulness of sin" (Heb. iii. 13). How constantly we have realised this! It is not merely the old story of *vanitas vanitatum*, but a case of direct, clear evil and suffering. Deceit is put upon us to lead us into sin. It is the apple in the garden over again.

Can we learn this in any way except by experience? Sometimes, it would seem that we cannot, and we give up the effort as regards our children. But let us not give up. We may save them from the danger if we can first make them trust us as real and not merely conventional guides, and, secondly, lead them to some experience of true good, of the happiness of love, charity, compassion, devotion. And we can save them from something of the deceits by which we have been deceived and have fallen, and teach them to use the world as not abusing it.

So we pray for them as well as for ourselves; it is not *me* but *us*. Yet I would not create the impression that we elder ones have done with these deceits. No, so long as our eyes open on the world, and our senses report the things of the world, we may still be deceived. But one day we shall see things οἷά ἐστιν in the day when all things are made manifest in the Light.

LECTURE III

We are still concerned with the amplification of the petition *Libera nos a malo*, and we come to prayer for deliverance from external dangers.

"From lightning and tempest; from plague, pestilence, and famine; from battle and murder, and from sudden death."

"From all sedition, privy conspiracy, and rebellion; from all false doctrine, heresy, and schism."

These are not moral evil, vice in the heart or in life; rather they are external calamities. Even sedition and false doctrine are here viewed as external to the supplicant. As to the concluding petition "from all hardness of heart", *duritia cordis*, that stands alone, and we shall treat it later.

In this enumeration of external calamities, especially of calamities due to the forces of nature, we are at once reminded of the early use of *Litanies* in the West, for processions in times of plague and famine. This was not their origin, for as I have said they began earlier in the East, and in the Liturgy; but they were early used in processions in time of special calamity. I read a passage from Hooker:

To the people of Vienna (Mamercus being their Bishop, about 450 years after Christ) there befell many things, the suddenness and strangeness whereof so amazed the hearts of all men, that the city they began to forsake as a place which heaven did threaten with imminent ruin. It beseemed not the person of so grave and reverend a prelate to be utterly without counsel as the rest were, or in a common perplexity to shew himself alone secure. Wherefore as many as remained he earnestly exhorteth to prevent portended calamities, using those virtuous and holy means wherewith others in like case have prevailed with God. To which purpose he perfecteth the Rogations or Litanies before in use, and addeth to them that which the present necessity required (*Ecclesiastical Polity*, Bk v. ch. xli. 2).

And an early English petition runs *a persecutione paganorum* where the Eastern Litanies had σεισμοί.

The Puritans objected that it was making perpetual what was only occasional, and general what should be particular. Hooker replies that Litanies

are of more permanent use than that now the Church should think it needeth them not. What dangers at any time are imminent, what evils hang over our heads, God doth know and not we...Such miseries as being present all men are apt to bewail with tears, the wise by their prayers should rather prevent. Finally, if we for ourselves had a privilege of immunity, doth not true Christian charity require that whatsoever any part of the world, yea, any one of all our brethren elsewhere doth either suffer or fear, the same we account as our own burden? What one petition is there found in the whole Litany, whereof we shall be able at any time to say that no man living needeth the grace or benefit therein craved at God's hands? I am not able to express how much it doth grieve me, that things of principal excellency should be thus bitten at by men whom God hath endowed with graces both of wit and learning for better purposes (*ib.* 4).

But besides lightning, tempest, plague, pestilence, and famine, there are three other ways mentioned in which danger to life is threatened; there is danger by the hand of man, death in fighting, death by treacherous attack, and there is death by accident. "Sudden death" is indeed not so understood generally. The objection often raised to the prayer for protection from sudden death may be very well defended on the ground of our unpreparedness. Again listen to Hooker.

Let us beg of God that when the hour of our rest is come, the patterns of our dissolution may be Jacob, Moses, Joshua, David; who leisurably ending their lives in peace, prayed for the mercies of God to come upon their posterity; replenished the hearts of the nearest unto them with words of memorable consolation; strengthened men in the fear of God; gave them wholesome instructions of life, and confirmed them in true religion; in sum, taught the world no less virtuously how to die than they had done before how to live (*E.P.* y. xlvi. 1).

But those who feel that they do not desire to pray against sudden death (and they are many) may very well take the petition in the sense of prayer against accidental death.

"From all sedition, privy conspiracy, and rebellion", etc. As the former dangers recall the troubled times of the later Roman Empire, so this group recalls the troubled times of the English Church. It comprises two series of three calamities ranged in an ascending scale:
"Sedition, conspiracy, rebellion;
false doctrine, heresy, schism".

Of these the two last in each pair were added in the time of Charles II.

In the New Testament the relation is reversed. "Schism" is used of the lesser divisions within the Church at Corinth, "heresy" of a more permanent evil. But this is not the case in modern times when "Schism" is the decisive, permanent division, a *rent*.

Then comes a sudden change to a Deprecation of a different character. The Litany turns back to personal sinfulness, and that in its worst and ultimate development, "hardness of heart", the final hardening, the result of persistence in sin.

As we began the list of sins with *caecitas cordis*, so now we end it with *duritia cordis*. None of the calamities recounted is so terrible as this. "Contempt of Thy word", associated with hardness of heart also in the collect for Good Friday, is a kindred condition. It is not so much the attitude as wilful disregard and disobedience.

It is the condition described in Heb. x. 29: πόσῳ δοκεῖτε χείρονος ἀξιωθήσεται τιμωρίας ὁ τὸν υἱὸν τοῦ θεοῦ καταπατήσας, καὶ τὸ αἷμα τῆς διαθήκης κοινὸν ἡγησάμενος ἐν ᾧ ἡγιάσθη, καὶ τὸ πνεῦμα τῆς χάριτος ἐνυβρίσας;

We pass to the *Obsecrations*. Here the Deprecations take a new form. Remember the sense of the Latin *obsecrare* = to adjure someone by something. *Oro per amicitiam* = I pray you in friendship's name.

The Obsecrations are so called because in them we beseech our Lord by the remembrance of all the acts of His Incarnate Life, the Economy of His Humanity.

The term however is not merely borrowed from Greek and Latin usage; it also comes to us from the Old Testament.

It is the character of the Psalms generally that they seek for deliverance by reciting God's former acts of deliverance, especially from Egypt; by reminding Him of them, pleading them, as it were. "Lord, where are Thy old lovingkindnesses?"

This Obsecration, which Israel addressed to Jehovah,

we address to our Lord Jesus Christ. We remind Him of His acts and His life, we obsecrate Him by them to hear us and deliver us from evil—*Libera nos a malo*. Scripture warrants us in so doing; we may quite reverently follow the analogy of human nature. Seneca says, a man will naturally say *non sustineo illum deserere cui dedi vitam, quem periculo eripui*.

There is then nothing superstitious in this Obsecration. It is going on human analogy, the higher instinct of Man, the teaching of Revelation. But it may of course be exaggerated as in the mediaeval Golden Litany where the grounds of obsecration are extravagantly multiplied.

But there is a totally different way of understanding and using the Obsecrations, and one which I suppose is more general because I find it preferred in ordinary modern notes and commentaries. I do not want to set it aside, or to say that it may not be combined with the way I have indicated. All I ask for is an effort of the mind to grasp its distinction. This other way of interpretation is that these acts of the Lord are mentioned as the means of our deliverance from evil, not as grounds of our pleading for deliverance. Let me set out this view. According to it we here ask Him to deliver us by virtue of these acts which have their continued efficacy. Now it is true that they have this efficacy, that we can expand them in this way, that it is proper so to consider them, and furthermore this expanded view of the means of our salvation is agreeable to the tendency of modern religious thought,

which declines to fix itself exclusively on the Atonement upon the Cross as the means of Salvation.
This is the view which regards the whole Life of our
Lord as the means of our salvation; it is the view taken
by Illingworth in his essay in *Lux Mundi*.

This is a true tendency and I am glad that it should
find expressions in the Litany which it can use in this
sense. All I am now contending for is that it is a
distinct interpretation, that it was probably not the
original interpretation, that if you adopt it you should
not lose sight of the other, and that you should recognise that it is distinct.

If you have any difficulty in this matter, I would
ask you to read Sir R. Grant's hymn:

> Saviour, when in dust to Thee
> Low we bow the adoring knee....

It may be made an objection that the last clause, "by
the Coming of the Holy Ghost", is not one of our
Lord's acts, and so cannot be pleaded to Him as such.
But although worded as *adventum* not as *donum*, yet
it is as our Lord's gift that the Church has ever
regarded the Descent of the Spirit. Cf. Luke xxiv. 49,
"Behold, I send the promise of My Father upon you".

After this by way of introduction let us consider the
verses in themselves; and let me say that the enumeration of the Divine acts loses a little force by combining
them together as in the modern Litany.

"The mystery of Thy holy Incarnation." We use
"Incarnation" of the whole economy of Christ's life
on earth; but here more strictly of the first step, of
His taking our flesh before His birth, as in Article II,

THE LITANY

"The Son...took man's nature in the womb of the Blessed Virgin". The collect for the Annunciation has the same strictly limited sense of the word: "As we have known the Incarnation of Thy Son Jesus Christ by the message of an angel...".

The word *incarnari*, "to be clothed with flesh", and the corresponding Greek are both founded on the one great expression in John i. 14, ὁ λόγος σὰρξ ἐγένετο, *Verbum caro factum est*. This is described as a mystery. Mystery in the New Testament sense is something not patent to human reason, but which can be received when revealed. It does not in the New Testament imply difficulty or *mysterium* in the modern sense.

But here "mystery" has both senses; it is something which has to be revealed and which when revealed cannot be understood.

The more one reasons about the Incarnation and its manifestation in the Lord's life, the more one feels that it is a mystery in the second sense. It is the union of the Infinite and the finite.

Of the other Divine acts only one or two are specified. The Circumcision is commemorated as bringing Him under the Jewish Covenant and obligation of the Law which He actually fulfilled.

It is this undertaking and fulfilling of the Law which makes the continuity of the two Covenants. There is no interregnum, no uncovenanted state. He fulfils the first while He brings in the second. And His example is a lesson as to human action. In all human movements of progress, religious or political, those have been most blessed in which the old has not been broken with, in which the central actors have presided continuously.

"By Thine Agony." "Agony" here has not the meaning in which we now use it of extreme pain, but of a particular kind of pain: the suffering which results from inward conflict. Conflict is indeed the fundamental sense. It was the conflict of the purpose of obedience with the weakness of the flesh. Τὸ μὲν πνεῦμα πρόθυμον, ἡ δὲ σὰρξ ἀσθενής. It is clearly no passing suffering which is described. And it is renewed in ourselves whenever we strive to bow ourselves to accept some sad message of coming disappointment, suffering, or death.

"By Thy precious Death...by Thy...glorious Resurrection." How much our devotion depends on the fitness and beautiful contrast of these two epithets, both taken from the Sarum Litany! "Precious death" perhaps comes from one of the Psalm passages, probably Ps. cxvi. 13, "Right dear in the sight of the LORD is the death of His saints". It was precious in the sight of God. Compare also the *Te Deum*, "Whom Thou hast redeemed with Thy precious blood", and I. Pet. i. 19, "The precious blood of Christ", which itself looks back to the same passage of Ps. cxvi.

LECTURE IV

Libera nos a malo. We have described the *malum*; we have besought for deliverance on the ground of all the redeeming acts. What more is there? There are special times when our need of deliverance from evil

is greatest. These are four. As to the "time of our
tribulation and of our wealth", I will only observe
that "wealth" here does not mean riches, but well-
being, the opposite of "tribulation".

But now consider the two last, "the hour of death, . . .
the day of judgment". We do not ask to be delivered
from them; they are inevitable. We look forward to
them, it is good to look forward to them. We answer:
it is not for deliverance from them that we pray, not
for protection in them. The cry is still, *Libera nos a
malo*, from sin and guilt. At such times the sense of
sin revives, with its hold on us and its terror and
behind it the terrible personality. *Libera nos a malo*.
There are two texts which answer these two petitions.
"In the hour of death." For this we are to take up
our Lord's words, "The prince of this world cometh
and hath nothing in Me". "In the day of judgment."
Hear St Paul: "I am persuaded that neither death nor
life . . . nor things present, nor things to come shall be
able to separate us from the love of God, which is in
Christ Jesus our Lord".

The Intercessions. The order of the Intercessions is
that of the Bidding prayer, "Ye shall pray for Christ's
Holy Catholic Church, and therein for the Church of
England". So here we have first the Church Universal
(and what "Catholic" means in the creeds that
"Universal" represents in the prayers). Then we go
on to the different estates, the King, the Royal Family,
the Clergy, Nobility, Magistrates.

The prayer for the Church militant is on the same
scheme, going indeed further than the Bidding prayer,

as it includes prayer for the suffering as in a later Intercession in the Litany.

Again compare the Prayer for all Sorts and Conditions of men. This was intended to represent the Litany when the latter is not used, and originally, besides prayer for the Catholic Church, contained prayer for the King, the Royal Family, and Clergy which now occur in separate collects; hence the word "*Finally we commend,* etc."

Intercession for the Sovereign. Here our Litany stands alone. It is not at first or chiefly for outward prosperity that we pray, but for the personal religion of the sovereign. There is nothing whatever about temporal prosperity in the first two verses; this only appears in the third. Certainly in our time[1] these prayers have been granted. Are we thankful enough for having over us a devout, believing Christian Queen of pure life and example?

For the Christian Ministry. Notice that the whole prayer concerns their relation to and use of the Word. This speaks of the Reformation which was in the minds of its best men a recalling of the Church and its teaching to New Testament standards. Notice further the prominence given to the Word in the Litany. We have already seen the contempt of the Word put forward as the last stage of sin. And again we ask for "increase of grace to hear meekly Thy Word", and again, "to amend our lives according to Thy holy Word" in the last supplication. Take three collects in which the Word is prominent; St Bartholomew, "Grace

[1] In 1896.

truly to believe and to preach Thy Word", "to love that Word which he believed". The collect is not wholly new, but "the Word" twice repeated is a Reformation addition. Again in the collect for St Andrew's Day, a Reformation collect which is entirely new, "called by Thy holy Word". Above all the collect for the second Sunday in Advent, "comfort of Thy holy Word". With this emphasis laid on the Word, compare the great change made by the introduction of systematic and sufficient lessons in place of detached sentences or unsystematic beginnings. See especially the second Preface, "Concerning the Service of the Church".

Notice also the emphasis on preaching and compare the words of the prayer for the Church militant, "that both by their life and doctrine", etc., where life and teaching go together. There, as is natural at Holy Communion, the administration of the sacraments is added to the other work on which we ask a blessing. But even there the prayer for the congregation is as to their hearing and receiving the Word.

For the Lords of the Council. This petition looks back to a time when the Privy Council as a body was of real importance and authority. In the seventeenth and eighteenth centuries its powers were concentrated in the Cabinet, which is in theory only an inner circle of the Privy Council. The powers of the Queen or King in Council are exercised by the Cabinet for the time being.

We still pray *for the Nobility*. It is a recognition of the existing social order which some of us value; and, whatever may be said, we all feel social influence.

"All Thy people." This may correspond to the Commons of the Realm in the Bidding prayer; but probably it is wider and refers to all Christian people.

"To all nations unity, peace, and concord." Here we step out into the wider circle of "all nations", not merely the Christian nations. The circle will be wider still when we pray for "mercy upon all men".

As to the *petenda*, "unity" means unity within, that internal unity which is better than alliances. "Concord" is a step beyond "peace".

"An heart to love and dread Thee." This and the following *petenda* are peculiar to the Reformed Litany, but the combination is already in the collect for the second Sunday after Trinity (taken from the Gelasian Sacramentary and founded on I. John iii. 20), "make us to have a perpetual fear and love of Thy Holy Name". It is the combination of the two, love and fear, which enables us to fulfil the commandments.

"And diligently to live after Thy commandments." The word "diligently" carries a lesson. It means "lovingly" (*diligo* = to love; the same word is the root of the English "delight"). It is only in love that we can keep the commandments fully and faithfully.

"Increase of grace", etc. This group of *petenda* is a good instance of the Biblical character of the new petitions. The general scheme of the petitions is from the parable of the Sower with its sequence "hear, receive, bring forth fruit".

"Meekly" is St James's word (James i. 21)—"receive with meekness the engrafted word". It is the absence, or rather the control of that disposition to challenge, question, or resist.

"Receive it with pure affection" comes from I. Pet. ii. 2, "desire the pure milk of the word". The "fruits of the Spirit" is from Gal. v. 22.

All this is dependent on Divine grace enabling for which we pray. The whole petition should be taken as a prayer before hearing the Lessons, the Sermon, or one's own family or private reading of the Bible.

LECTURE V

Now come four Intercessions for the special needs of others, (a) spiritual, and (b) temporal.

"That it may please Thee to bring into the way of truth", etc. This expresses the true attitude towards doctrinal error, and one which the Christian Church has often failed to understand or adopt. It is not the persecution or compulsion, but intercession for the erring. And observe the charitable interpretation. The leaders are the *errantes*, the followers are the deceived, the πλανώμενοι.

The Intercession is addressed on behalf of corrupt or imperfect forms of Christianity; it will scarcely apply to the heathen. And we cannot but regret the absence from the Litany of missionary supplications. We may not adopt Hooker's line of defence. It would be sad if the experience of more than three hundred years had not produced in us a deeper sense of our duties, a deeper desire of service which might well be expressed in special intercessions. Of course that sense and that desire have grown, and it is, we must confess, a serious defect in our Prayer Book that we should have scarcely anything more than the petition for all men, to which we shall come in a moment, and five or six words in the Prayer for all Sorts and Conditions of Men. There was a missionary intercession in Bishop Hermann's reformed Litany, "That Thou wilt send forth faithful labourers into Thy harvest". It is a pity that this was not embodied in our Litany.

"That it may please Thee to strengthen such as do stand", etc. This second Intercession for special needs is a very beautiful and complete one. It is mainly due to Hermann's Litany. And when we speak of Hermann's Litany, we must remember that it was really the work of Melanchthon and Bucer, framed on the model of a Litany by Luther himself. It is through Hermann's book that the Continental Reformers influenced our Prayer Book, and the influence is really that of Luther by way of Hermann.

In this Intercession notice again the method of the Litany in each verse as well as in the whole. Those who are standing, those who have fallen, and between them the weak-hearted. "Such as do stand" comes from I. Cor. x. 12, "Let him that thinketh (in relation to temptation) he standeth take heed lest he fall".

"Them that fall." How thankful we are for this petition! The word "fall" is very rarely used in this sense in the Bible. It is part of the great metaphor of the Way for the Christian life of which *The Pilgrim's Progress* is the English exponent.

Between these come "the weak-hearted", *pusil-*

lanimes. It is the exact rendering of ὀλιγοψύχοι in
I. Thess. v. 14 (a word which had been taken up in
Greek literature), those in danger of becoming
δειλοί. These are represented by Feeblemind in *The
Pilgrim's Progress*, Part II. It is not however mental
but moral feebleness that is intended—the irresolute,
the yielding, the timid.

Then comes a last petition for something far beyond
the other three. It is borrowed from Rom. xvi. 20:
ὁ δὲ Θεὸς τῆς εἰρήνης συντρίψει τὸν Σατανᾶν ὑπὸ τοὺς
πόδας ὑμῶν ἐν τάχει, "And the God of peace shall
bruise Satan under your feet shortly". That verse
itself is but the taking up of the primal prophecy
against the serpent in Genesis, "it (i.e. the seed of the
woman) shall bruise thy head", fulfilled first in Christ,
and then in each of us. Does not this inspire us with
a new encouragement for the next conflict with the
Tempter?

Now come the two Intercessions for special, temporal
needs. "That it may please Thee to succour", etc.,
"to preserve all that travel", etc. On the first of these
I will only say this, that it is specially one of those
prayers which have meaning for those who are making
the endeavour to help others by personal ministration.
If you are day by day visiting, helping, encouraging,
and feel the inadequacy of your words and the in-
sufficiency of your help, with what earnestness and
comfort will you turn to the prayer that He will bless
and do the work through you or without you!

"To preserve all that travel." Now we fall back
on the Greek. The phrase is taken almost word for

word from the very ancient Liturgy of St Chrysostom. So you see, the Prayer of St Chrysostom which ends our Morning and Evening Prayer is by no means the only link between the Litany and the ancient forms of the East. There is abundant evidence that St Chrysostom was closely studied by our Reformers.

For the dangers of travelling in old days it is enough to refer to St Paul's text in II. Cor. xi. 25. And yet we are glad to have the prayer for the far less frequent and imminent dangers of modern travel. And this petition has often endeared the Litany to those who are anxious for others on the road. There is a very beautiful quotation in Comber[1] from the Liturgy of St Basil: τοῖς πλέουσι σύμπλευσον, τοῖς ὁδοιποροῦσι συνόδευσον, "Sail with those who sail, journey with those who journey". It is a petition resting on the memory of the storm on the lake when He stilled the winds, and of the journey to Emmaus when unrecognised He "drew near and went with them".

"Prisoners and captives (i.e. prisoners of war)." No clause has so long a history. It takes us back so far, back to first beginnings, to the earnest prayer of the Church for Peter. The prisoners mentioned in early liturgical forms are Christians, prisoners διὰ τὸ ὄνομα. For such prisoners prayer was offered in obedience to the injunction of Heb. xiii. 3, μιμνήσκεσθε τῶν δεσμίων ὡς συνδεδεμένοι, "Remember them that are in bonds, as bound with them". And "remember" means remember in prayer and in service.

In the Epistle of St Clement to the Corinthians, lix,

[1] *History of Liturgies*, by T. Comber (1690), pt I, p. 152.

there is a kind of short Litany almost metrical in the original Greek, and it has this clause: λυτρῶσαι τοὺς δεσμίους ἡμῶν, "Ransom our prisoners". So, later, prayer was to be made for τῶν ἐν μετάλλοις, "Slaves in the mines".

Here then we are taking up and carrying on the ancient prayer which was offered in the Church of Asia for Ignatius on his way to the lions, in Vienne for Blandina, in Carthage for Perpetua and Felicitas.

There may be at this moment, there certainly have been not long ago, δέσμιοι διὰ τὸ ὄνομα in our own day. But we may give a wider interpretation, and pray for prisoners, not διὰ τὸ ὄνομα, but for their own faults—moving thought and care for these.

"The fatherless children, and widows." Again the Reformers went to the old Greek sources. There is the strongest evidence of the care of widows and orphans in the early Church. Widows are frequently mentioned in the New Testament. There are special regulations for them in I. Tim. v; widows and orphans are named together in James i. 27, "Visit the orphans and the widows". The Apostolic Fathers abound in references to the care of widows and orphans. It is a note of heretics that they neglect widows and orphans (Ignatius, *ad Smyrn.* 6). All this had been taken over from Old Testament teaching, where in very many passages widows and orphans are regarded as being specially under God's protection.

So here as elsewhere we have the Church beseeching God to assist and prosper it in a duty which was felt to be specially according to His will.

"The desolate and oppressed" seem to represent the stranger of the Old Testament who was liable to oppression and was especially under God's care. Compare Deut. x. 18.

"Have mercy upon all men", lest any should be left out under the particular headings.

It is strange to us that there should ever have been objection taken to so scriptural and beautiful a petition. But there *was* an objection strong enough for Hooker to deal with it specially. It was said, "If we know that all men cannot be saved, that there are many who are not elect, is it right to pray for what cannot be?"

Without arguing the point we are content to rest in the words of I. Tim. ii. 1 and 4, "I exhort that supplications, prayers, intercessions and giving of thanks be made for all men"; "Who will have all men to be saved, and to come to the knowledge of the truth".

[At this point notice the intentional omission of prayer for the dead which stood here in the Sarum Litany, "Ut omnibus fidelibus defunctis requiem aeternam dones". Surely this omission makes the intention of the framers of the Litany perfectly clear.

"Forgive our enemies, persecutors, and slanderers." Our Lord's injunction in Matt. v. 44 was literally carried out in Justin and in the early Liturgies. The practical point for us is the petition for our slanderers, i.e. for those whom we know or believe to have spoken unfairly or unkindly of us.][1]

The last two verses of this portion of the Litany are

[1] Crossed out in the MS.

still intercessions, but they more distinctly include ourselves.

"Give" and "forgive" expand the Lord's Prayer, and the former occupies in the Litany as relatively small a space as the prayer for daily bread occupies in the Lord's Prayer. Certainly the special connexion of the Litany with the Rogation Days is not strongly marked, at least in our form of it.

"True repentance." The final prayer is for forgiveness and renewal. And here once more note the reference to God's holy Word.

I take only one point—the mention of "negligences and ignorances", and of these especially the latter.

The word here means sins of ignorance or inadvertence. It is not used in the Old Testament but only in the Apocrypha, and there three or four times, e.g. Tobit's prayer.

But there is much about sins ignorantly committed in Lev. iv and v, and there is an express prayer for pardon of them in Ps. xix. 12, "Who can discern his errors?" i.e. sins of ignorance. "Clear Thou me from hidden faults", not hidden from others, but hidden from myself.

In Old Testament times with a far-reaching ceremonial law of clean and unclean penetrating every relation of life, it was impossible to avoid transgressing through ignorance. But is that so still, now that the ceremonial law is gone? Yes, the Law of Christ, the Law of Love, is equally penetrating and far-reaching, entering into all the relations of life. How certain it is that we have offended, and shall offend, inadvertently, yet sinfully.

[Sins of ignorance are sins if the ignorance is voluntary, if we do not seek to know in all things. But if we have sought to know, and do endeavour to know, then there is no prayer for forgiveness which we can use with such confidence as this, that He would for Christ's sake forgive us our ignorances.][1]

LECTURE VI

"Son of God: we beseech Thee to hear us." This passage down to the end of the Lesser Litany is to be taken as pressing the preceding Intercessions, in the spirit of importunate prayer, enjoined by our Lord in parable, and recommended by His own example; compare the Syrophenician woman, and blind Bartimaeus.

At this point we begin to feel strongly the method and arrangement of the Litany, which hitherto seems only to result in a certain sense of confusion. Few of us, I suppose, could write out the Intercessions in actual order. The cause is that they are derived from so many different sources. I shall try and help you to see the order. To do this and at the same time to bring out the devotional side of the study would require two more lectures, and I have only one. So I am compelled reluctantly to-day to confine myself to criticism and explanation almost to the exclusion of devotion. Yet I hope that what I say will indirectly tend to a more profound devotional use of the Litany.

[1] Cancelled in MS.

THE LITANY

The *Agnus Dei*. This is an independent hymn, used not only here but in other places. Anciently it was threefold, with three different responses, *exaudi, miserere, dona pacem*.

"Lamb of God." Of course the reference is to St John Baptist's words in John i. 29, Ἴδε ὁ ἀμνὸς τοῦ Θεοῦ, ὁ αἴρων τὴν ἁμαρτίαν τοῦ κόσμου. There the singular is used, ἁμαρτίαν; sin is thought of in its unity, a grander view than the plural suggests.

And the expression "Lamb of God" means the Lamb provided by God: Gen. xxii. 8, "And Abraham said, My son, God will provide Himself a lamb".

This name is not often used in the Prayer Book, so it is all the more striking in the Commendatory Prayer for a sick person at the point of departure: "Wash it, we pray Thee, in the blood of that immaculate Lamb, that was slain to take away the sins of the world".

Then comes the *Kyrie* or *Lesser Litany*, introductory to the Lord's Prayer. We have the same use in Morning Prayer and in Evening Prayer and in four occasional Offices, Marriage, Visitation of the Sick, Churching of Women, and Burial. It is to be regarded as addressed to the Trinity. So, like the Invocation at the beginning of the Litany, it brings in the thought of the Three Persons, and is in prayer what the *Gloria patri* is in praise.

The *Lord's Prayer*. You will notice here the absence of the doxology. This was the uniform custom of the Western Church and it no doubt correctly represents the original text of Matt. vi. 13. The doxology, or

125

rather the doxologies, were very early liturgical additions used in the East, and in the East only. Our Reformers took up this doxology and added it in certain places where there is praise, e.g. in the first Lord's Prayer and in the Lord's Prayer after Reception. Elsewhere, as here, they did not add it.

It was not that they believed themselves bound by the text of St Matthew, but they felt the force in its proper place of the joyful conclusion. We are fully entitled to use the prayer both with and without the doxology.

From the East also they took the custom of audible recitation, "with a loud voice", and of the people joining in.

As in Morning and Evening Prayer the Lord's Prayer is followed by versicles. But only two are selected out of several which came here in the Sarum Use. These two are from one verse in Ps. ciii, "He hath not dealt with us after our sins; nor rewarded us according to our iniquities". It is worth while noticing the influence of the Psalter not merely in whole Psalms but everywhere in thought and phrase.

Oremus. Perhaps you have wondered why this occurs in the middle of prayers here and further on. The cause lies in the clear distinction between two kinds of prayer: (1) *preces*, and (2) *oratio* or *collecta*. Hitherto we have had *preces*. Now a continuous prayer recited aloud. *Oremus* reminds the people that they have a part, though they do not join in aloud. So again when the next set of *preces* is ended, the Minister says *Oremus*. The responses to the Commandments are also of this character, so there the Prayer for the Queen is introduced by *Oremus*.

"O God, merciful Father." An ancient collect. I only notice the word "assist" which here and elsewhere means "be present to hear", not "help us in praying". Compare the collect at the end of the Communion Service, "Adesto, Domine, supplicationibus nostris".

Now comes a rather difficult and complicated section: "O Lord, arise" to end of the *Gloria patri*. This is from the Rogation Monday Litany in the Sarum Processional. It is really a Psalm with an Antiphon preceding and succeeding and a *Gloria* following. All this is obscured by the fact that instead of a whole Psalm (Ps. xliv), it was directed in the Sarum Processional that only one verse should be said, and that direction is retained in effect. To men as familiar with the Psalms as mediaeval clergy the initial verse of a Psalm would suggest the spirit and thought of the whole Psalm. That spirit and thought are exactly suitable here. It is a cry for deliverance in time of extreme suffering and oppression, and it is founded on former *magnalia*, "noble works". So we should regard it and use it, trying to call up the memory of the past.

As to the *Antiphon*. I cannot enter now into its various significations. But there is one with which you are acquainted in our Cathedral Commemoration Services.

An antiphon is a sentence from the Psalm which is being sung, or from some other Psalm or other part of Scripture. So here, "O Lord, arise" is repeated before and after the verse with a slight variation: "Name", "honour". This is really v. 26 of the same Ps. xliv, only taken from a different version. After the second repetition of the antiphon, the *Gloria* follows which belongs to the Psalm.

Now come eight versicles addressed to Christ from another of the Sarum Litanies. *Si necesse fuerit versus sequentes dicantur a clericis in tempore belli*, runs the rubric. Traces of warlike times are everywhere, not only in the Hebrew Psalms, but in Christian liturgical forms. Compare the collects for Peace in Morning and Evening Prayer. It is incorrect to look on the latter as only a prayer for spiritual peace.

As to the versicles themselves I will only remark that *Fili Dei* (Sarum) is changed into *Fili David*. Why? I can only guess. But the address made by Bartimaeus in all three accounts is ἐλέησον υἱὲ Δαβίδ.

"O Lord, let Thy mercy be showed upon us." This is from another source, Ps. xxxiii. 22, hence it is divided between the Priest and people. It is also found as the last verse but one of the *Te Deum*. Then comes another collect, "We humbly beseech Thee, O Father", half of it old, half of it Cranmer's work, one which must often in time of trouble have struck us as especially beautiful; personally, I feel much more drawn to it than to the earlier collect.

Let me take this opportunity of speaking on the deprecatory character of the Litany as a whole. It gained that character not from its origin in the Eastern Church, but from its use in the Western Church. It is well to realise that it is drawn up largely with that view. Perhaps you are accustomed to think of it as simply penitential, suitable to Lent, etc. It *is* penitential in and under and occasioned by external suffering. Hence at times we have a feeling of its being inappropriate.

I return to the collect "We humbly beseech Thee". The first part, like the former collect, is from an ancient prayer. But that prayer was one to turn from us our evils "*omnium Sanctorum tuorum intercessione*". Not only did Cranmer omit this, but he endeavoured to neutralise the association by emphatically stating the contrary doctrine. There is an intentional force in the words "our only Mediator and Advocate", founded on I. Tim. ii. 5, εἷς καὶ μεσίτης Θεοῦ καὶ ἀνθρώπων, ἄνθρωπος Χριστὸς Ἰησοῦς, "One mediator between God and men".

The same reason, viz. the character of a previous collect, accounts for "our only Mediator and Advocate" in the collect for Saint Stephen's Day.

The Prayer of St Chrysostom. I have already spoken of its origin. The prayer affords the most marked instance of what holds in less measure throughout the Litany. It is Cranmer's own translation and it occurs here for the first time.

It was not till more than a hundred years later that it was added to the end of Morning and Evening Prayer.

The Grace. This is often described as a blessing, but it is really just as much a prayer as the preceding collect.

Every blessing is a prayer, but not every prayer is a

blessing. This sentence as St Paul uses it is a blessing. He says, "Grace be with you", but here the Minister says, in the name of the congregation, "Grace be with us".

So we end our Litany as we began it with the doctrine of the Trinity, not so much as doctrine but as being a source of consolation and joy.

We began with an invocation of the Trinity to pity poor sinners. Here we have risen to a higher and more hopeful approach. We no longer merely plead for mercy; we do not hesitate to ask confidently for those peculiar blessings which are associated with the work of each of the Divine Persons. We do not hesitate to ask for them for us all, and to ask for them for ever.

II. HYMNS AND HYMN WRITERS[1]

I. EARLY NON-METRICAL HYMNS

The first effect of the descent of the Holy Ghost at Pentecost was that the assembled believers speaking in many tongues glorified the μεγαλεῖα Θεοῦ. It was an outburst of praise. That was the beginning of Christian Hymnody, in the many languages of the earth. At first, no doubt, it was chiefly the Psalter which supplied the material. In it sounded the praises of Messianic and Christian hopes, and such were very probably the hymns which Paul and Silas sang in prison at Philippi. But as the proportions of Christian Faith dawned more fully—the Incarnation, the Atonement, the Resurrection, the doctrine of the

[1] Salisbury Cathedral, Lent, 1900.

Trinity—something more explicit was needed, and the Christian faith produced its own proper hymnody.

Hence these Christian doctrines are the topics of praise in the earliest hymns. The first external testimony is that of Pliny the Roman governor, who speaks of Christians singing hymns to Christ as God.

In what languages shall we find the earliest relics of this lost primitive treasury of praise? There are two languages in which we find remains of the earliest Christian literature, Syriac, and Greek. Latin for the present is out of the question, for Latin Christianity was entirely derived from Greek, and as yet had no independent existence.

There is no Christian literature in Latin till long after the apostolic age; an obvious illustration of Greek being the language of the Christian Church is the Epistle to the Romans, written in Greek. Not before the end of the second century did Christian writers write in Latin.

But to return. We may put aside the Syrian Church. It did produce hymns, still extant, and earlier than Greek, but we need not concern ourselves with them to-day. It is Greek hymns which claim our first attention, and happily we still possess, and still use, two very ancient Greek hymns to which I will direct your attention, before we take the *Te Deum*, which in its extant form at least, is not Greek, but Latin. These two hymns are non-metrical, and here some explanation must follow. Our idea of a hymn would be an address to God in praise, or prayer or confession, and that it should be (1) in metre, and (2) in rhyme. But the early Greek hymns are neither in metre, nor in rhyme. Rhyme in poetry does not establish itself till well on in the middle ages—and so it is not found in Greek hymns at all, in early Latin very sparingly, and not till mediaeval Latin, really established. The two Greek hymns of which we are speaking to-day are not merely not in rhyme, but not in metre. They read like prose in their original language. But in their case probably there is in the arrangement of words and syllables an adaptation to musical rendering, though not amounting to metre.

Now let us come to the actual hymns themselves.

(1) Φῶς ἱλαρόν, "Hail, gladdening Light" (*Hymns Ancient and Modern*, 18), the oldest hymn in the book, and certainly third century, for Basil in the fourth century speaks of it as an ancient song, and does not know the author. Our rendering is happily by Keble.

First, we must realise the occasion—it is an Evening Hymn. It is sung at the lighting of the lamps for Vespers, and this gives the suggestion for addressing Christ as Φῶς ἱλαρόν. There is a touch of the same appropriateness in "Lighten our darkness" in our Evening Prayer.

It is a hymn to Christ—He is the Φῶς ἱλαρόν, but it is a Light from Light (as in the Nicaean Creed, and in Heb. i. 3, "the brightness, or effulgence of the glory of the Father"). "Heavenly, Blest", and "Holiest of Holies", belong to the Father.

Then the hymn gives the moment—"Now are we come to the sun's hour of rest". "The lights of evening" are not the sunset, but the lamps within the church. Then the Trinity—that great doctrine which it had been the work of the Greek Church to clear and define. Finally we turn specially to the Son, "to Whom, not now only, but at all times it is right to sing with holy voices".

Why should we not silently remember, and offer praise and prayer, when cheerful light comes into our own room, as we sit at work? It is as fit then as in church.

(2) *Gloria in excelsis.* Though known to us only by its Latin title, it is Greek. You will at once remember it as the hymn of praise in the Communion Service, after Reception.

In the Liturgy before the Reformation, no thanks, nor praise, were provided for communicants after Reception. Simply, the congregation is dismissed. But when, in the Reformation, actual participation was made the great point in the service, the Gloria was transported from the earlier part to the end; and it has been suggested that the words of Matt. xxvi. 30, "when they had sung a hymn, they went out", may have influenced the Reformers.

But though in its Latin form it has been long associated with the Holy Communion, that was not its original use in the Eastern Church from which it came, nor is it so used there to-day. It was, and still is, the *morning* hymn of the Greek Church.

As to its great antiquity: it is found at the end of the Greek manuscript of the Greek Bible, Codex Alexandrinus, written in the fifth century. It would never have gained such a place, unless already very ancient.

It begins, as you see, with the song of the angels, and then turns to praise of God the Father. Next follows a paragraph of prayer to Christ—an *Agnus Dei* somewhat like that in the Litany—founded, of course, on John i. 29. Then it ends with the praise of Christ. Here the Holy Ghost is mentioned, but it is certainly an interpolation, and one which spoils the reference to Phil. ii. 11, "That every tongue should confess that Jesus Christ is Lord, to the glory of God the Father".

In Greek hymnody, the attitude of the poet is always one of self-forgetful, rapt, or ecstatic contemplation. While in the English hymn the body of the hymn consists of the human blessings, warnings, or enlightenments which flow from the subject taken, the mind of the Greek hymn-poet rests, and delights in the revelation itself.

The contrast is most marked in the absorbed rapture with which the Greek poet hymns the Divine perfections and the Incarnation, as compared with the self-regarding character of our praise. That is to be seen in some degree in *Gloria in excelsis*. You will scarcely trace it in hymns from the Greek in *Hymns Ancient and Modern*, as for the most part they are not really translations, but original hymns from which a suggestion has been taken.

(3) Now we pass to the *Te Deum*, from Greek to Latin. This also is not in metre, either in Latin or English. Yet even here it is not quite certain that we have not, in part of the *Te Deum*, an ancient Greek hymn. It is very probable that verses 1–10 are a translation from Greek, and that the rest of the hymn, so far as original, is Latin.

But it is not, and never has been, used in the Eastern Church as far as we know.

We must dismiss the attractive tradition about Ambrose and Augustine at Augustine's baptism. It is a compilation, a hymn which has grown. That is the distinction between sacred and profane poetry (except perhaps Homer), that sacred poetry has grown. One of our finest hymns, "Great God, what do I see and hear", is the work of several authors, gradually built up, and improved.

Next, as to age and use. Our Bishop fixes it early in the fifth century, and the South of France.[1]

A question has often been raised whether the whole hymn was originally addressed to the Second Person of the Trinity, and *Te Deum* looks like this. But we have to do with it as it now stands, in English, and the first thirteen verses are addressed to the Trinity in Unity, as may be seen by verses 11, 12, and 13.

Now as to the divisions. Verses 1–13 are Praise to the Trinity, 14–20 is a Creed, 22–end are versicles.

In division 1, notice the widening circles—Apostles, Prophets, Martyrs, and finally, the Church.

Secondly, what I have called the Creed. Notice how closely parallel it is with the Apostles' Creed—the Sonship, the birth from Mary, the Death, Resurrection, Session at the Right Hand, and the Coming to Judge, and prayer added (to Christ).

Thirdly, the Versicles. Prayer is based on faith in Christ's nature and work. It is to be noticed that, of

[1] Cf. *The Te Deum, its structure*, etc. by Dr John Wordsworth. S.P.C.K. (2nd ed. 1902).

the last eight verses, seven are from Psalms—not always recognisable, because they are taken from Latin versions, with which our versions do not always agree. The one exception is very beautiful and precious: "Vouchsafe, O Lord: to keep us this day without sin". It is borrowed from a longer form of the *Gloria in excelsis*, of which we spoke before. It is a very humble prayer, yet a lofty one.

I must just mention something as to its special uses. It is an important part of our Coronation Service; we can remember it at our Jubilee Service. It has also been used in the Western Church to thank God for great and exceptional blessings, especially national ones.

There are the lines in Shakespeare's *Henry V*, spoken by the English king after the victory of Agincourt, when the roll of the dead has been brought in:

> Do we all holy rites:
> Let there be sung *Non nobis*, and *Te Deum*.

II. LATIN METRICAL HYMNS

A

More than 300 years have passed since the praises of the Church at Pentecost before the Latin-speaking Church begins its offering of hymns. So far as we know, it was at Milan under St Ambrose that the singing of hymns in the manner of the Eastern Church was first adopted in the West. There may have been similar endeavours in Gaul, which always had intercourse with the Eastern Church independent of Italy—but they were insignificant compared with the work of

Ambrose at Milan, and at any rate we have comparatively little evidence with regard to them.

Ambrose introduced Eastern Church music—of that I have nothing to say, interesting as the subject is —but besides introducing music, he provided words. He was the first conscious Western hymn writer; we have twelve of his hymns at least—one of which (*Splendor paternae gloriae*, *Hymns A. & M.* 2) in translation has taken some hold on the English Church: " O Jesu, Lord of light and grace ". There is an excellent criticism by Archbishop Trench (*Sacred Latin Poems*, p. 86), "no softness, little tenderness, a rocklike firmness"—you can hardly realise the truth in the English version, as the ruggedness of the originals is more or less softened in the translation. From a critical point of view they are prosaic—just what one would expect from a practical man of action like Ambrose. And yet they were the beginning of a great stream of sacred poetry, and had power at the time to move deeply.

That they *did* have this effect we have contemporary evidence, that of the great Augustine. Ambrose was his spiritual father, and under his influence he regained faith. And it was Ambrose who baptised him. Compare *Confessions*, Bk IX. cc. vii, viii. These hymns and music were *Ambrose's* hymns and music, introduced by Ambrose. Not only this passage but scattered references to extant hymns show the power which they were exercising.

Next, let us take two from another soil, and different in character—more florid—*Hymns A. & M.* 96, 97;

these are sixth century, and from France. (1) *Vexilla Regis prodeunt*, "The Royal Banners forward go"; (2) *Pange, lingua*, "Sing, my tongue, the glorious battle".

The first was the welcome of Fortunatus to a supposed fragment of the true Cross, sent by Justin II to the convent at Poictiers, on November 19, 569. Hence, throughout, the Cross is the subject, and the hymn is a processional. So taken, it has interest and even grandeur. The first line is the finest, and accounts perhaps for its surprising popularity. The second line at once introduces the subject: "The Cross shines forth in mystic glow". But I think the conceit about the Cross with two arms being like scales, on which price was weighed must seem frigid and artificial. There is the same artificiality in Fortunatus's other great hymn, *Pange, lingua*. Stanzas 2 and 3 are far-fetched, and still more is "Bend, O lofty Tree", etc. What we have a right to ask of a hymn is that it should move us of itself—not that it should present riddles difficult to unravel—and Scripture riddles were what many early Latin hymn writers delighted in.

The next three are of a much higher character.

(1) Take first *Veni Creator*. This is the only hymn which our Book of Common Prayer retains. Our Matins and Evensong were made up of the old offices, but in the compilation the hymns which they contained were dropped. This hymn was retained in the Ordinal. The second of the versions,

> Come, Holy Ghost, eternal God,
> Proceeding from above...

is the oldest by more than a hundred years, and I am sorry to say it has quite dropped out of use. It is no doubt a paraphrase, rather than a version, but it is much more faithful, and it brings out points which have been omitted, e.g. stanza 3:

> In faithful hearts Thou writ'st Thy law,
> The finger of God's hand.

In the original the Holy Spirit is called *digitus Dei*. The first version was added in 1662 and may have been by Bishop Cosin. Compared with the original, it is not at all a close version and is, I venture to think, even finer than the Latin.

(2) "O Strength and Stay" is a very ancient hymn for the ninth hour; allusion is made to the changes of the day. It is crabbed and difficult in the Latin. Of this, you will notice, we have two translations, *Hymns A. & M.* 11 and 12. The latter thoroughly modernises the original, but with so much grace and tenderness that we may give it a high place.

(3) "Jesu, our Hope, our heart's desire" (Ascension Day, *Hymns A. & M.* 150), probably seventh or eighth century.

This is one of the best of the early hymns, and it possesses simplicity, directness, and strength. There was no need to add a modern doxology. I must complain of the way in which *Hymns A. & M.* have disfigured old hymns with third-rate doxologies, so that the last verse, which ought to be the strongest, is the weakest.

And here I ought to pause and notice the great reluctance of the Roman Church to adopt and use

these hymns. They first found a home in the Bene-
dictine monasteries in the seventh century, and it was
there that they came regularly into use at the hour
services, and it was from monastic use that they gradually won their way into the churches, and became an
acknowledged element in services. Later, in the
thirteenth century, we have a sufficient proof of the
hold they had on the popular mind in the frequent
and beautiful allusions to some of them in Dante's
Divine Comedy.

B. *Mediaeval*

This is the most fertile period; I have only taken
very few of the best known.

(1) "Jesu! the very thought is sweet", "Jesu, the
very thought of Thee" (*Hymns A. & M.* 177, 178).
Iesu dulcis memoria. In this, you will at once see the
very different character. We have come to hymns of
the affections; we are in an atmosphere of mystical
religion—the religion of the *Imitation of Christ*. This,
and the Jerusalem hymns of Bernard of Clairvaux, are
of the same character. In one, the affections go out to
the Person of the Lord, in the other to the Life to
Come.

Undoubtedly this is a hymn which is a real help to
devotion; how far it is suitable for general congregational use is another question. Neither of the two
versions gives us more than a fragment; it is a long
hymn of about fifty verses.

Side by side with it in the *Hymns A. & M.* is 176,
John Newton's hymn, "How sweet the Name of
Jesus sounds", and a comparison is natural, I suppose.

To some the English, to others the Latin, tone of devotion will appeal most. But, again, the aim and purpose of both are the same.

(2) "Brief life is here our portion" (*Hymns A. & M.* 225). These are extracts from *De contemptu mundi*, a poem of 3000 lines by St Bernard of Cluny (c. 1140). Dr Neale, to whom we owe our translation, says of it: "The greater part of the poem is a bitter satire on the fearful corruptions of the age, but as a contrast to the misery and pollution of the earth, the poem opens with a description of the peace and glory of heaven, inspired by the last chapters of the Apocalypse".

So far as these hymns paint for us the new Jerusalem in its symbolic beauties, they are for all ages. But there is another side to all these hymns of the cloister—there is a contempt, and despair of the world and its activities, and a religious pessimism which, to-day at any rate, is not natural, wholesome, or real. I do not say you find it in these extracts, but it is characteristic of the poems as a whole, and it does set the tone of the other mediaeval hymns—and this I think we should avoid.

Bernard's hymn leads the way in a great company of the hymns of the new Jerusalem, of which we have noble examples in English.

Sequences.

There is another class of mediaeval Latin hymns which, though to all appearance hymns, have another name. We begin to hear of these in the twelfth century, and they are very numerous. To tell how they arose and their difference from hymns, would detain us too long. But the most evident distinction is their position. They were sung not in hour offices, but at Mass, between the Epistle and the Gospel, where until then there had only been a prolonged Alleluia with musical notes unprovided with words. These musical notes without words were very difficult to remember, and it was to meet this difficulty that Notker wrote his Sequences. I believe that in Sequences the melody was not repeated as in hymns, but continued to vary throughout. Hence these Sequences were appropriate to the Mass used on particular days: *Dies Irae* to All Souls' Day, *Stabat Mater* in Passion Week, and "The strain upraise" (*Hymns A. & M.* 295) in Epiphany.

(1) *Dies Irae.* I do not hesitate to give it the first place. It combines awfulness and tenderness in a way which no other hymn does. It is absolutely untranslatable. You will remember three stanzas in the *Lay of the Last Minstrel*: "That day of wrath", sung by the monks of Melrose at the end of the poem. This is a condensation rather than a translation; in the record of Sir Walter Scott's last days his biographer says, "We often heard distinctly the cadence of the *Dies Irae*". I have spoken fully on this subject on a former occasion, so I need not dwell on it now[1].

(2) *Stabat Mater.* This hymn has a great history of affection and devotion in the Latin Church, and as you read it you may perhaps be surprised. I do not think the English version has ever made any great hold.

[1] Cf. a course on the *Dies Irae* delivered in Advent, 1899.

(*a*) It has suffered by translation in respect of rhythm. In the Latin it is a marvel of beautiful rhythm, that we necessarily lose.

(*b*) It appeals to those to whom the Blessed Virgin Mary is a constant (I might say, a principal) object of devotion. To such worshippers her sorrows appeal. It is indeed in the latter verses a prayer to her, to enable us to feel as she felt in contemplating the Cross. It is one which an English Churchman cannot honestly recognise, or reproduce, but, if the purpose of the hymn is altered, its power to move is gone.

(3) "The strain upraise." This is of course modelled on Ps. cxlviii, but it has sufficient independence not to be accounted merely a version. It is one of those hymns of pure praise, which form the most important gain which we owe to Dr Neale and others who have translated Latin hymns.

At the beginning of the present century, this element was one which English hymnody lacked, and *Hymns A. & M.* have supplied it. Yet one feels that it is an element which needs to be kept within limits. For simple words of praise which do not evolve or invoke any *thought*, can never form the staple of hymnody for a thoughtful people, though they are an element which cannot be dispensed with.

C. *Modern*

I have not left myself time to speak of these. I will only correct an error into which we might naturally fall.

When we hear that a hymn is from the Latin we naturally think of it as ancient. This is by no means the case. Many very beautiful Latin hymns were composed in France in the seventeenth and eighteenth centuries, by Coffin and others, and a considerable proportion of the French hymns in *Hymns A. & M.* are translations of hymns of that date. No. 479, "Great God, Who, hid from mortal sight", is a spoilt translation of a very grand hymn. Compare the unaltered form in an earlier edition, and the short evening hymn, "As now the sun's declining rays" (13), which is perfect—two stanzas, each with a complete thought, and the doxology.

On the whole, the service done by *Hymns A. & M.* is considerable.

They have, as I said, reinforced the element of pure praise. They took advantage of the work of men like Neale, Chandler, and Elleston, whose translations had not before met with much acceptance.

They restored a link between the Church of England and the early Church, which was broken by the excision of the ancient hymns from our services at the Reformation. They have shown us the way and the degree in which we can be in sympathy with mediaeval religious thought, and have enabled us to realise our Catholic position. But, in my opinion at least, they have gone too far. The Latin element is too strongly represented in the collection. Many of the translated hymns have no particular merit or power to move the soul. Or if they seem to have such a power, they owe it to their tunes, rather than their words—a kind of influence which the greatest of the Latin fathers, Augustine, in a well-known passage vehemently deprecates.

In an English hymn book, I cannot but think the national element should strongly preponderate, if it is to appeal to the mass of ordinary worshippers. And I think one may fairly say that, with a very few glorious exceptions on the Latin side, the best English hymns excel in poetry and devotion the best Latin hymns, whether you regard the latter in their translations or in their original tongue.

III. GERMAN HYMNS

To-day I labour under a special disability. Our debt to Germany as regards hymnology is even more for music than for words, and on that I am unable to speak, except to say that, to me, their solemn chorales are very impressive. It is remarkable that several of the German hymn writers were also composers.

Another difficulty is that German hymns are comparatively little known. It is true that Miss Winkworth's *Lyra Germanica* is fairly well known among the educated—a friend told me that for many years they sang these hymns at their family prayers on Sundays. But they are little known in the Church of England. *Hymns A. & M.*, which occupies the ground, gives only a few. You will see that among the representatives chosen on the list only two are in *Hymns A. & M.*, and I cannot but attribute this to a narrow prejudice against Luther and the Protestant Reformation. You will find a greater proportion in other collections. We should clearly understand that congregational singing is entirely due to the German Reformation.

No doubt, one reason for so few coming into general use is the excessive length of German hymns. Ten stanzas of eight lines each is a very common thing in the Lutheran hymn books.

I say Lutheran, because it is to the Lutheran Protestants of Germany, not the Reformed or Calvinists, that we owe German hymns. Among the Reformed in Germany, as in Scotland and France, Calvin's view was maintained that only the Scriptures should be used, and it is only in the last twenty years that hymns have been generally used in Church services in Scotland, and, indeed, in England. We owe the beginning of the change to Wesley.

I do not think this is to be deplored or spoken of with ridicule. The result has been that the Psalms, or their Scriptural Paraphrases, have set the character of English hymnody.

The feeling against hymns in relation to Scripture grew out of a reasonable Protestant reaction against the mediaeval hymns with their legendary allusions.

However, let us return to the Lutheran hymns. And here I must remark that German hymns have a currency outside Germany. A great proportion of the hymns in use in the churches of Sweden, Finland, Denmark, Norway, Iceland, are translations of German hymns which lend themselves easily to translation into these cognate languages.

One more point, by way of general introduction. German hymnology is in relation to what goes before, and what follows.

There were German translations of Latin hymns

before Luther, and Luther himself began by translating. Again, there is a close connexion with England. Through the Moravians, John Wesley became acquainted with German hymns, and translated many, e.g. the translations, "Commit thou all thy griefs", "Lo! God is here", "Jesus, Thy blood": these are all by John Wesley.

Let us now come to the hymns which I have selected as typical, or rather on account of their special positions in the land of their birth—though this does not apply to all.

The first that meets us is familiar to some of us as a Christmas carol, either in its original form or in a translation, "Good Christian men, rejoice". It is certainly pre-Reformation.

It is one of those Macaronic hymns that is in two languages, half Latin, half German—in our version, half Latin, half English. The quaintness of this gives it a charm, but besides its quaintness, it has a real simple beauty, and depth of childlike feeling.

Leaving this, we come to Luther. Luther's hymns were (1) songs of conflict, and (2) songs of doctrine. They were the outcome of his great work, and weapons for it; and very powerful they are. One needs to know and understand Luther, in order to enter into his hymns. He was strong, fearless, convinced, rough, coarse, violent: yet tender and loving, a marvellous compound. Take a sentence from his table-talk, "I love the second Psalm with all my heart, it strikes and flashes valiantly among kings, princes, councillors, and judges".

(1) The first of the two hymns to which I wish to draw attention, "Ein feste Burg", is a song of conflict: a song of the man who stood up alone against Emperor and Pope. You see where the inspiration comes from —Ps. xlvi, "God is our hope and strength: a very present help in trouble". It is not a metrical version, but it starts from the thought. The Psalm is the calmness of retrospect, "The Lord of Hosts is with us: the God of Jacob is our refuge".

Luther's hymn breathes more of the conflict. I must not attempt its history, not tell how it was sung at Diets, and on battlefields—on the field of Lützen, before the great victory in which Gustavus Adolphus died for the cause of the Reformation.

(2) There were also hymns of doctrine: "Nun freut euch, Christen", "Be glad now, all ye Christian men", is distinctly doctrinal.

It is a soul's history of finding salvation, indeed, it is Luther's own. It probably had an immense effect. If it can scarcely be called a hymn, a close examination would refuse that title to many hymns of to-day.

"Christ lag in Todesbanden", "In the bonds of Death He lay", is truly a hymn, a noble Easter hymn, written on the best Latin models, and purely objective. It is marvellous that it should not have come into common English use in Miss Winkworth's noble translation.

Nicolai. "Wachet auf", "Sleepers, awake". This hymn is familiar to us through Mendelssohn's *St Paul.* The composer has taken Nicolai's Chorale, and words. It is of course a song of the parable of the ten virgins.

Only we must notice that, besides the first stanza, there are two more in Nicolai's hymn almost equally beautiful. You will find the whole hymn in *Lyra Germanica*. It is said to have been written in time of terrible pestilence.

"Nun Danket", "Now thank we all our God" (*Hymns A. & M.* 379). This is the next best known. Again, like Luther's, this had a historical setting. It breathes hopefulness, when the miseries of the Thirty Years' War were drawing to an end, and freedom of conscience was close at hand in the Peace of Westphalia.

It is taken, as you know, from Ecclus. l. 22–24, except of course the Christian doxology of the third stanza.

To understand its position, see Ecclus. xliv onward.

First the introduction: "Let us now praise famous men...". Then, xliv. 16, the list begins, and it goes on with Old Testament worthies ending with Simon the Priest. Then our verses are the Epilogue of praise for all God's dealings with the nation.

Electress Luise.[1] "Jesus meine Zuversicht", "Jesus my Redeemer lives". This hymn is little known, but to me it is the most attractive of all. It is the Gospel of the Resurrection, and preaches the Risen Lord as the trust of the soul. Everyone who can read German ought to read and learn this hymn; Miss Winkworth's translation, in *Lyra Germanica*, First Series, is good, but it *is* a translation.

Gerhardt, the psalmist of the love of God to man. His hymns are more subjective, and represent varying

[1] Louise of Brandenburg, foundress of the Orphan House at Oranienburg.

moods. His own life was sad and trying, and involved in the controversies between Evangelicals, and Reformed, and his hymn is expressive of this.

"Befiehl du deine Wege", "Commit thou all thy griefs". He shows us where, and how to do so, and this has, I believe, been more than any other hymn a fountain of comfort to those who are seeking for relief.

As far as I know it is not included in Miss Winkworth's collection. There is a fine translation of it by John Wesley in the Wesleyan hymn book—I can commend it to you—and also in the new Scotch *Hymnary*.

Tersteegen. If a subjective character of hymn appears in Gerhardt, this is far more manifest in Tersteegen. In him we find a thorough mystic. He lived apart, and separated from all Church communion, and was resorted to from all sides for special counsel. You can see the mystical character from a hymn given in *Hymns A. & M.* (600)—"Thou hidden love of God". You see it is headed for a Retreat, or Quiet Day, and is quite unsuited for congregational use.

There is however a finer example, for which again we are indebted to John Wesley. It is "Lo! God is here!" (*Hymns A. & M.* 526).

Read it in German or English, and you will acknowledge that, as has been said, Tersteegen had an intense power of realising the unseen. He does seem able to put us as we read in the felt presence of God.

Zinzendorf. I have chosen one of his many hymns to remind us of the Moravian Church of which he is one of the chief figures.

You will find in Miss Winkworth's *Christian Singers* or in many other books the ancestry of the Moravian Church—its strange wanderings, its extraordinary missionary zeal, its abounding hymnody. We should never forget what missions owe to the example of Moravia. I have already mentioned that it was through the Moravians that German hymns first came to Wesley, and they formed the inspiration of Wesleyan hymnody.

The last hymn of which I have to speak to-day, "Tender Shepherd" (*Hymns A. & M.* 402), has no pretension to stand side by side with the others in force, depth, or popular recognition. Still, I could not help mentioning it, and I can never read it without being touched. It comes from a well of pure, simple feeling. This is the note which the author prefixes in his own edition: "Sung in four parts beside the body of my little fifteen-months-old son, Johannes Ladislaus".

It has been so translated by Miss Winkworth that one can hardly believe it a translation. It is so simple, and has such pathos.

I shall have attained my object to-day, if I lead some of those many among us who read and study German to turn to German hymns for devotion. Surely, more mutual understanding of inner religious life—less holding apart from Lutheran communion—would do something to recover that lost feeling of blood relationship between us and the German nation.

IV. ISAAC WATTS AND CHARLES WESLEY

Now we turn from Greek, Latin, and German, to English. We value the contributions of other times and lands, their history and associations give interest; but it is the voice of the piety of our own race, our own forefathers, which will always touch most surely the hearts of the mass of English Christian people.

And this voice is late in coming. In Germany, the voice of Protestant hymnody awoke at the Reformation, and, as we saw last Friday continued to pour forth its praises through the sixteenth and seventeenth centuries. In England there was nothing corresponding to this. The English Reformation had but little Church Song; in place of hymns they had metrical versions of the Psalms. The first of these, the Old Version, appeared in part in the reign of Edward VI, but was not complete till 1562.

We still know it by its hundredth Psalm, "All people that on earth do dwell".

It was followed nearly 150 years later by the *New* Version, in the reign of William and Mary, which held its ground as the Church Song-book for more than a hundred years, and may still be seen printed in old prayer-books.

Isaac Watts. Not till the beginning of the eighteenth century do we come to the father of English hymnody, Isaac Watts. There were various causes for this—chief among them was the strong influence of Calvin's school, and their objection to the use of anything except the Psalms in the Church Service. Hence the Old Version and New Version held their ground.

There had been sacred poets of a high order, Herrick, George Herbert, and Henry Vaughan; but not hymn writers.

Sacred poems and hymns are distinct, as we see clearly enough in the case of Keble. Very few of the poems of the *Christian Year* could be sung in a congregation. The most notable exception to this absence of hymns is the publication in 1695 of Bishop Ken's three hymns written for the school of Winchester; though I do not, of course, mean that there were no others, e.g. "Jerusalem, my happy home".

The honour of leading the advance of English hymnody is due to Watts, and the honour of receiving and using it, to the Independents to whom Watts belonged, and to the Nonconformists (or Congregationalists) generally. Both the earliest writers of English hymns whom we take to-day represent the Nonconformists; for, though Charles Wesley continued till death in the communion of the Church of England, he was a Methodist preacher, and it was out of the Wesleyan movement, and in support of it that his great contribution to hymnody was produced.

I have taken only these two names for our consideration to-day, but we must remember that they are followed by other names of men who have contributed hymns of nearly equal merit—Doddridge, Cennick, Oliver, Perronet, names perhaps unfamiliar, though their hymns are well known to you.

But to return to Isaac Watts. He was a Southampton man. There is not time even to sketch his uneventful, retired history. He was a man of most pure, devout life, of great tenderness, gentleness, and charity. He was full of deep humility, and a thorough scholar and student. I will begin by professing warm admiration for Watts—I put him in the first rank.

It is of course true that, in the large mass of hymns which he wrote, many are open to severe criticism, but there are many much greater poets of whom much the same thing is true; some of you will remember Matthew Arnold's criticism on Wordsworth.

There are hymns of Watts in which we find grotesqueness, prosiness, bad taste, defective rhyme—and the faults of the time and of his contemporaries in exaggerated forms. And these blemishes sometimes mar a stanza in the midst of his very best hymns.

Besides all this, there is the effect of the narrow Calvinistic doctrine in which he was bred; the dwelling repulsively on the vengeance of God, the malice of Satan, the depravity of man, and further, in certain hymns we find too much freedom and familiarity in the expression of affection towards the Saviour; a fault which is also to be found in the very opposite school, and in such men as Faber.

But, keeping all this before us, we still feel that Watts was a *poet*—that much of his work is of the highest order.

It is a weak kind of piety which cannot put up with a homely word or a bad rhyme for the sake of the devotion and fervour which overflow it.

Watts's work falls into two divisions, half entitled hymns, half psalms.

As I have said, English Protestantism (and especially the Calvinism in which Watts had been reared) was strong in its adherence to the Psalms as the proper vehicle of Christian praise.

Watts took in hand to make the Psalms express Christian praise, to impregnate them with Christian thought, and to bring the Gospel into them, not merely to put them into metrical form as in the Old Version and New Version. And it was a thoroughly justifiable endeavour. Was the Christian Church to go on praising God for the same blessings which the Jewish Church had used? Might not the framework of the Psalms, especially of the predictive Psalms, hold and sustain our praises for the Redemption of the Cross, and for life eternal ensured by the Resurrection? Watts's own title-page expresses his idea—"The Psalms of David, imitated in the language of the New Testament, and applied to the Christian state, and worship".

Let us take a simple, obvious illustration (others you can find for yourselves). Psalm lxxii is a Psalm relating to Solomon, or, at any rate, to the reign of an ideal Hebrew king. But Watts boldly begins, "*Jesus shall reign where'er the sun*".

There is another point to be noticed about Watts's versions. They are not *complete* versions, like the Old Version and New Version; they take a *portion* of the psalm, expand it, and bring it out. So with the most famous of all his hymns, "O God, our help", if

you compare Watts's full text with Ps. xc, it does not
go beyond six verses. I say full text, for the form
generally used is only a selection. It is chiefly the
verses expressing God's eternity, and its support to us,
that are taken. Watts's three verses on human transitoriness are omitted; one is a very fine one, it is this:

> The busy tribes of flesh and blood,
>   With all their lives and cares,
> Are carried downwards by the flood,
>   And lost in following years.

It is easy to see, in studying these versions, that Watts
was a good Hebrew scholar who knew what the
Psalms meant.

My own impression is that his Psalm-versions are
his best work, better than his hymns, and one reason
why is obvious: he had the thought supplied to
him. Ps. xc, of which I have just spoken, stands
almost at the head of all lyric poetry, sacred or profane.
What Watts had to do was to enter into the spirit of
the Hebrew, and clothe it in simple, direct, vigorous
English; and this he has done as no one else before or
since.

Simple, direct, vigorous English: this is, I think,
the character of all the six hymns which we are
engaged upon, and not only of these, but of many
more.

We must now pass to his original hymns; though
even these are not original in the sense of being independent of Scripture—they are full of it.

The greatest of his hymns is "When I survey the
wondrous Cross". It is natural to compare it with

other hymns on the Passion, e.g. *Vexilla Regis*, or "O sacred Head, surrounded".

In Watts's hymn, there is no detailed dwelling on the pangs and wounds, the humiliation and desolation. There was indeed one stanza approaching that character, which is now always omitted.

But Watts's hymn is one of peaceful contemplation, deeply moved but tranquil, and it is subjective, strictly so—the feeling of the individual. But there is nothing in that to unfit it for a congregation, for it is the feeling of all—all under the same emotion, the same impression.

Then there is much thought in it—the thought is St Paul's thought, expressed in the Epistles to the Philippians and Galatians—the glorying in the Cross, the sense of the worthlessness of all else compared with it:

> Love so amazing, so divine,
> Demands my soul, my life, my all.

And then, instead of leaving us resting in that solemn thought, *Hymns A. & M.* must needs interrupt with a trivial commonplace verse of their own, because, forsooth, hymns must have a doxology at the end of them!

If one is to mention the strong points in the teaching of Watts's hymns, they are, I think, these:

1. First, of course, his grasp of the Atonement. He does indeed lay hold of the pardon of Christ, and helps us to do so.

And yet in his confidence there is no presumption

—it is in humility and deep consciousness of our infirmity:

> My soul looks back to see
>   The burdens Thou didst bear
> While hanging on the accursed tree,
>   And hopes her guilt was there.

2. His realisation of the hope set before us of the heavenly land, and the dwelling with God, as in "There is a land of pure delight".

3. His belief in the Communion of Saints, and in the consolation of this in bereavement. His funeral hymns stand high among his other work, as for instance "Why do we mourn departing friends".

You may read his best in *The Book of Praise* of Lord Selborne, who has recognised Watts's merit in ungrudging measure, but I must myself read you one which I think specially fine (*Hymns A. & M.* 623):

> Give me the wings of faith to rise
>   Within the veil, and see
> The Saints above, how great their joys,
>   How bright their glories be.
>
> Once they were mourning here below,
>   And wet their couch with tears;
> They wrestled hard, as we do now,
>   With sins, and doubts, and fears.
>
> We ask them, whence their victory came:
>   They, with united breath,
> Ascribe the conquest to the Lamb,
>   Their triumph to His Death.
>
> They mark'd the footsteps that He trod,
>   His zeal inspired their breast;
> And, following their incarnate GOD,
>   They reach'd the promised rest.

Our glorious Leader claims our praise
    For His own pattern given;
While the great cloud of witnesses
    Show the same path to Heaven.

Charles Wesley. I am now going to speak of Charles Wesley, though I fear I have left little time for him.

I have already said that, though a member of the Church of England, he is to be taken in connexion with the Wesleyan movement. His hymns are rightly looked upon by Wesleyans as embodying their aspect of Christian doctrine.

Yet, in coming from Watts to Wesley, we feel in a more ecclesiastic atmosphere. The influence of the Latin hymns is evident. Hymns of praise are more numerous, and more joyful, and his hymns admit of being arranged and adapted to Christian seasons. To him we owe hymns for Advent, Christmas, Easter and Ascension Day.

Yet, taking Charles Wesley's hymns on the whole, they have too much of an extremely valuable element, that of personal experience, experimental religion. To deny such an element a place in hymns would be not only wrong, but absurd, in the face of the Psalter, which contains so much of it. But a hymn for general use should be capable of carrying a congregation with it, and evidently many of these hymns cannot. There are, of course, some phases of experience so common and necessary that hymns expressing them will always meet with response, a response perhaps at first weak and feeble, but nourished by the hymn itself, and growing in volume.

Take two of Charles Wesley's hymns:

1. His greatest—"Hark! the herald-angels sing". It is a hymn which is the justification of hymn menders. It has been undoubtedly improved:

> Hark how all the welkin rings
> Glory to the King of Kings.

And again:

> Pleased as man with man t'appear
> Jesus our Immanuel here.

Again, four very inferior stanzas at the end are now never heard.

In its present form it is perhaps the finest hymn of praise in the language. It is as objective and as dogmatic as any of the earliest Latin hymns, and withal it is true poetry.

2. Now let us turn to another great hymn: "Come let us join our friends above".

Here the hymn menders have been less successful. They have permanently deprived us of the trumpet call of Wesley's first verse:

> Come let us join our friends above
>   That have obtained the prize,
> And on the eagle wings of love
>   To joys celestial rise.

You will find the true text with all the omitted stanzas in Lord Selborne's *Book of Praise*.

If we are to compare Watts and Wesley, I think we may say that Wesley is smoother in versification, and that his rhythm is better.

He is more modern in style, and nearer our generation, but I doubt if he has quite so much vigour as Watts.

What I feel about both, though in different measure, is the conviction, the special force, which breathes in their hymns.

The nineteenth-century hymns are melodious, refined, pathetic, devout; but they seem to me to lack the force and unction, the power of the Spirit, which is in these hymns of the eighteenth century.

In conclusion, I must refer to a poem of Charles Wesley's, not a hymn, though it is printed as one in the Wesleyan collection, a poem, now, in our days, coming to be more recognised as of first-rate merit. No one can estimate Charles Wesley's powers till he has read his great lyric, "Come, thou traveller unknown".

V. NEWTON AND COWPER

Last time I spoke to you of the beginnings of English hymnody.

It was the Nonconformists' contributions which occupied us exclusively, and especially Watts, who led the way.

To-day we will discuss the contributions of two friends, both Church of England men, but in line of thought and tone closely akin to Watts.

The hymns of Newton and Cowper appeared in a joint volume, at one time largely read, now seldom seen, named *Olney Hymns*, from the small Buckinghamshire town of which Newton was curate, and in which Cowper resided at the time.

In the preface Newton explains its purpose ; a desire of promoting the faith and comfort of sincere Christians, though the principal, was not the only motive to this undertaking. It was likewise intended as a monument to perpetuate the remembrance of an intimate and endeared friendship.

They were two very different men. Newton's character was strong, manly, and sound. Cowper was delicate and sensitive.

So Lord Selborne in his criticism contrasts the manliness of Newton's hymns with the tenderness of Cowper's; and yet Newton was not wanting in tenderness.

Again, Newton was no poet, whereas Cowper afterwards, not at the time of the Olney hymn-book, but later, produced *The Task*, which obtained for him a permanent and important place in the history of English poetry.

But the two had this in common: that both had in youth led godless lives—both had been converted, had turned from darkness to light; both carried with them the deepest sense of former guilt, and of the mercy of God in bringing them to repentance and peace. Of course, even here in the similarity, there was a difference. Newton's life, in his youth, had been actually profligate; Cowper's was never that, but quite godless, idle, and dissipated.

Again, with Newton, the sense of acceptance never faltered, and to the end of his life he was a happy, active, earnest servant of God. With Cowper it was broken in upon by madness, and, through the last twenty-seven years of his life, he never recovered religious peace, but believed himself cast out from God's presence. This, however, did not affect his hymns, which were all written before this last period of despair.

John Newton. But I must return to Newton. Consider what he was, entirely self-educated, and that under the strangest circumstances, a sailor from boyhood, the commander of a slave-trade sloop on the Guinea coast, converted, ordained at the age of thirty-nine, placed in a miserable, impoverished, degraded parish, in which he laboured with untiring zeal.

This is the man from whom those admirable hymns which I have quoted on the paper in your hands come, besides many others which perhaps are most readily accessible in Lord Selborne's collection.

There are many others in the Olney hymn-book which are the merest prose put into rhyme. No doubt you will be disappointed, not to say surprised, if you take up the older hymn book itself. Many so-called hymns are short sermons. Indeed he heads one division "Solemn addresses to sinners", apparently quite unconscious that a hymn is different from a sermon. Others are reflections, meditations, inquiries.

But there is this about all of them, it is honest and sincere work. In part the prosaic character of Newton's hymns was intentional. He himself lays it down that "in hymns, the imagery and colouring of poetry, if admitted at all, should be admitted sparingly, and with great judgment". It is the opposite extreme to the hymns of Dean Milman, of which I shall speak next time, and still more to the style of modern English hymns, in which ornament of language is so much sought for.

On the whole, though it is a wrong position, it is far the best of the two extremes. A plain, unadorned expression of genuine religious emotion is, I believe, the true character of a good hymn. But it needs some poetic power to give that plain expression so as to reproduce it in the heart of another.

Let us now attend to Newton's greatest hymn, "How sweet the Name of Jesus sounds" (*Hymns A. & M.* 176). It is natural to compare it with St Bernard of Clairvaux's *Iesu dulcis memoria*, of which I spoke when we were dealing with Latin hymns. To make the comparison fair, we want the Latin. To me it seems that the national character of the Frenchman, or rather the Burgundian, on the one side, and of the Englishman on the other, comes out clearly.

The Frenchman is more emotional, more vehement, and, in the later part, too unrestrained. The Englishman is not less deep in his affection but there is a calmness throughout.

The words are weighed, and not less strong because they are weighed. If there is less emotion, there is more thought: there is that orderly progression which we saw was wanting in *Iesu dulcis memoria*. It clings more definitely to the thought of the Name, and hence, because less vehement, more measured, it is distinctly more fit for congregational singing.

What can be better than the last two lines?—

> And may the music of Thy Name
> Refresh my soul in death.

Next take "Glorious things of thee are spoken" (*Hymns A. & M.* 545), a real hymn of joy and praise. It is true there are few such in the Olney hymn-book, but this is compensation. You will say that here is poetical ornament; true, but the poetry is from Scripture. He gathers from all parts—Ps. lxxxvii, Is. xxvi, Ps. xlvi—and yet the effect is not that of a cento; there is a natural unity. What can be finer than the form in which he presents Ps. xlvi. 4: "There is a river, the streams whereof make glad the city of God"?

> See! the streams of living waters,
>   Springing from eternal love,
> Well supply thy sons and daughters,
>   And all fear of want remove.
> Who can faint, when such a river
>   Ever flows their thirst to assuage?
> Grace, which like the Lord, the Giver,
>   Never fails from age to age!

Notice how in the last stanza the individual element comes in. That is the differentia of Newton's hymns —he will not contemplate the glory of Zion without turning to the thought of his own personal share in relation to it, his share in it.

Lastly notice another hymn, or rather poem, in which again we find the same touch of poetry. It is seldom in collections and so I will read it.

> As when the weary trav'ller gains
>   The height of some o'erlooking hill,
> His heart revives, if 'cross the plains
>   He eyes his home, though distant still.

While he surveys the much-lov'd spot,
  He slights the space that lies between;
His past fatigues are now forgot,
  Because his journey's end is seen.

Thus when the Christian pilgrim views,
  By faith, his mansion in the skies,
The sight his fainting strength renews,
  And wings his speed to reach the prize.

The thought of home his spirit cheers,
  No more he grieves for troubles past;
Nor any future trial fears,
  So he may safe arrive at last.

'Tis there, he says, I am to dwell
  With Jesus in the realms of day;
Then I shall bid my cares farewell,
  And He shall wipe my tears away.

Jesus, on Thee our hope depends
  To lead us on to Thine abode:
Assur'd our home will make amends
  For all our toil while on the road.

It is a simple, natural image, which touches the most ordinary mind; and what beauty and grace of treatment, coming not from art, but from true feeling.

William Cowper. It is impossible here to give a sketch of Cowper's tragical life, but I must say enough to put his hymns in their right place in it. As the hymns of an eminent English poet, they must with a few great exceptions cause disappointment.

There are many in the *Olney Hymns* in which lie little or no merit. It is a strange exception to common literary history that Cowper's real poetic power did not develop till he was past fifty years of age; and his hymns were written before that development. The hymns belong to the happy, peaceful period between his two great attacks of insanity, *The Task* and his other poems to the period between the second attack and his death. This latter period, so fruitful in other ways, could produce no hymns, because, although in every other respect he recovered from that second attack, he was still insane in one particular respect—as to his religious conduct. He believed that God had willed him to commit suicide, and that for not doing so he had been irrevocably condemned, and was hopelessly lost (that is expressed in *The Castaway*). Thus the very power of addressing God in praise or prayer was taken away, just at the period when his poetical power had come to its late maturity.

Hence the surprise with which one finds that, with a few exceptions, Cowper's hymns are not superior to Newton's—they are perhaps even inferior.

"Jesus! where'er Thy people meet" illustrates Cowper's relation to Newton. It was composed when Newton's weekly prayer meeting, in which Cowper often took part, was moved to a larger house. Like very many of these, it was distinctly based on Scripture, the first two verses direct from Ps. lxvi. I said Cowper was not superior to Newton but this is a notable exception to the rule. Here Newton and Cowper are side by side.

Let us now take Cowper's best known—"Hark, my soul! it is the Lord". It seems to have been the custom for the two friends to take the same subject. So, here it is our Lord's words to St Peter, *Amas me?*

Newton first: he gives us for a hymn what is really the notes of a self-examination—sincere, frank, earnest, of great interest and value, but certainly not a hymn, as we can gather from the very first line, "'Tis a point I long to know".

How differently Cowper takes it. He is bold—some might say too bold. He expands the Lord's question "Lovest thou Me?", puts the words into the lips of the Saviour. He makes the words, while in form a question, really a gracious appeal to help and move the cold heart. It is always a perilous thing to give human words to Christ. But how worthily and scripturally has Cowper done this! The words are really the reflection of his own experience of the love of Christ to himself. Yet how peaceful the retrospect is.

Then at the end, just one verse of answer, no more, yet containing all that can be said. It is a verse which has dwelt in many minds.

Take another hymn, even more a hymn of expression than "Hark, my soul", "O, for a closer walk with God", wisely classed in *Hymns A. & M.* (630) as for Mission Services and Instructions, as it is certainly not suitable for ordinary congregational singing.

Cowper's hymns have been criticised as being too distinctly experiences, too peculiar to his own case. But surely the sense of having grieved the Spirit, of having lost close communion and spiritual comforts, is *not* a peculiar experience, but in some degree common to almost all real Christian life.

"There is a fountain fill'd with Blood." Let us remember at the outset that, like the last, this is a hymn on a text—"In that day there shall be a fountain

opened...for sin and for uncleanness", and also Rev.
vii. 14, "they washed their robes, and made them
white in the blood of the Lamb".

But even so this is a hymn which, I doubt not,
many will positively dislike. There are expressions all
through it which a refined, cultivated taste cannot
altogether approve, and especially is this the case with
the first stanza. But, to my mind, the intensity of the
feeling redeems all this.

And I feel certain that a great proportion of our
congregations, especially those of the working class,
would have no such feeling, and that these expressions
would be for them quite natural and full of force, and
merely counterpart of the Scripture.

It is a hymn of prayer for the Atonement, one of
many in the *Olney Hymns*, but the fullest, most
definite, most personal of them all—and, I venture to
think, of very real value—able to *move*, which is
what we want for a congregation.

There is an unfortunate alteration in verse 2—
"may I", for "have I". Cowper meant it for a thanksgiving for cleansing, and forgiveness already definitely,
fully received—and not a thanksgiving for a possibility.

There are two more hymns of quite a different
character—songs of joy and thankfulness, in a subdued key but a sustained one.

The first, "Hear what God the Lord hath spoken",
a melodious little hymn from Is. ix, which certainly
ought to be, but is not, in common use. The other,
"Sometimes a light surprises", is full of grace and
beauty of expression, gathered from both the Old and

New Testaments, first from the Sermon on the Mount, and then from that lovely and seldom-read passage at the end of Habakkuk—let me at least quote that one concluding verse:

> Though vine nor fig-tree neither
>   Their wonted fruit shall bear,
> Though all the fields should wither,
>   Nor flocks nor herds be there;
> Yet God the same abiding,
>   His praise shall tune my voice;
> For, while in Him confiding,
>   I cannot but rejoice.

You may perhaps still think that I have given the Olney hymns more prominence than they deserve in this brief review of hymns. I will not take a testimony from the Evangelical writers in the Church of England, whose piety they nourished, but from outside. I will quote this person's exact words: "The author himself can remember the Olney hymns acting like a spell on him for years, strong enough to be for long a counter influence to very grave convictions, and even now to come back from time to time, unbidden into the mind". Those are the words of Frederick Faber in his preface to his own hymns, which he intended to be for English Roman Catholics what the Olney hymns had been for himself in his boyhood.

VI. BISHOP HEBER, AND LATER HYMN WRITERS

Heber. To-day we pass to nineteenth-century hymns, and such a multitude of writers! But a little careful consideration shows plainly and decides for Heber as the leader, and in some measure as a representative.

The value and amount of Heber's contributions would perhaps hardly justify this remark. But his work was a turning-point.

In his day, hymns were beginning to be introduced into parish churches, and there for the most part Watts, Wesley, Newton, and Cowper were all of course identified with one section of the Church. Indeed there were hardly any others. Naturally enough, hymns were regarded with disfavour by the High Church of the day and by the authorities of the Church generally, and further, the use of hymns at all, instead of Psalms, was looked on as irregular and unauthorised.

This is how Heber speaks of it in writing to Bishop Howley: "The evil, if it be one, of the admission of hymns into our churches, has spread so widely that it would be wiser to regulate the liberty, than to take it away". That is how he feels obliged to speak when he is trying to get recognition.

Again, he says in a letter to a friend: "I have been for some time engaged in collecting, correcting, and arranging my hymns, which, now that I have got them together, I begin to have some High Church scruples against using in public".

Well, that was the state of things. And Heber's endeavours form a turning-point, in this way:

(1) He writes and selects hymns which shall follow and fit the calendar of the Church. The title of the collection is *Hymns written and adapted to the weekly Church Service of the Year*. They were intended to be connected with the collects and Gospels, and to be

sung between the Nicaean Creed and the Sermon. That is his account. It is so familiar to us now, that the idea of a hymn book on any other plan seems almost strange.

This plan gives the collection a Church of England tone; and, being made in this spirit, opened the way. Not only so, but coming from a man so universally loved and admired as Bishop Heber, it received impetus. There had been slight and obscure attempts before, without making any great improvement.

(2) A second point is the distinct abandonment of a tone, hitherto prevalent, of too great familiarity, too little awe. On this point Heber felt very strongly. Presenting his own tentative verses in 1811 he claimed that in them "no fulsome or indecorous language has been knowingly adopted.... It is not enough...to object to such expressions that they are fanatical; they are positively profane...." The brutalities of a common swearer can hardly bring religion into more sure contempt, or more scandalously profane the Name which ·is above every name in heaven and earth, than certain epithets applied to Christ in some of our popular collections of religious poetry." This is very sound and true. It is a protest which might very well be made over again with regard to Faber's hymns, and also to some translations from Latin hymns, now largely in use.

(3) The beginning of a new style of hymn, in which rhetorical and poetical ornament is largely adopted. This has gone on to our own day. Here, there is much that might be criticised, both in Heber

and Milman, and their successors. Probably Newton's canon is the rule—of which I spoke last time.

I have given you roughly the conditions and character of the new movement represented by Heber. But it is worth your while to trace this more fully. You will be able to do so in Dr George Smith's excellent *Life* of Heber.

You will see there that directly he began parish work he became conscious of the need, first to inquire, and then to write.

In the letter quoted above, he sought encouragement, and authorisation. This he received, and was going forward to publication, when suddenly the Bishopric of Calcutta called him away. This prevented publication, and his collection was not printed till after his death in 1827. This little volume which I have here, by the kindness of the Dean,[1] is the second edition, published in the same year as the first.

You will see that it was the scheme, the spirit, the method, the person from whom it came, and the fact that nothing of the same sort had ever been produced before, that gave this little book its importance in the list of English hymnals.

Now we may turn to individual hymns. At once we notice that they are not all by Heber. Fifty-seven are by Heber, twelve by Milman (afterwards Dean), and there are twenty-nine from other sources.

(1) Let us take the first, "Holy, Holy, Holy! Lord God Almighty!" (*Hymns A. & M.* 160)—the best known,

[1] George David Boyle, Dean of Salisbury from 1880 to 1901.

which we have just sung. It is, like so many of the best which we have examined on previous days, a free paraphrase from Scripture, Rev. iv. 8–11.

Notice how he lets the song of the four beasts suggest the metre—the first line is unaltered, and he adapts the rest. The great merit of this hymn is that it concentrates our thoughts throughout on God, and keeps them there.

It is an utterance of pure praise, it does not seek to penetrate, or explain. The darkness hides God. This fits the day. On Trinity Sunday we feel we are in face of a great mystery. Notice how beautifully the two epithets "Merciful" and "Mighty" come in. Then the thought of the Trinity is in "Perfect in power, in love, and purity".

(2) "From Greenland's icy mountains" (*Hymns A. & M.* 358). It is impossible to estimate what this hymn has done for the missionary cause. It has moved and stirred great multitudes, and been the means of giving spirit and life to many a little country gathering in tent or barn. It stands with "Jesus shall reign", and "All hail the power", as one of the three great English hymns, and it is, to the taste of many, first of the three.

It is, like all Heber's hymns, ornate, but in moderation, not more than enough to attract. It is elevated in thought, and yet plain, easily intelligible. It rises as it goes on, and the fourth stanza forms a grand climax. That is a great point in a hymn, and by no means common. It is perhaps a little unfortunate that it should begin by naming a land to which we have never sent missionaries, but no doubt the story of

Hans Egede, the Danish missionary, had reached him, as I daresay it has some of you.

(3) "The Son of God goes forth to war" (*Hymns A. & M.* 439). Here we have one of the earliest, if not actually the earliest, English hymn for a Saint's Day. It has brilliant poetic power, and comes to us from one who left brilliant prospects at home, and gave himself up, to die from the effects of fever, and overwork, at the age of forty-three. The spirit which speaks in it is the soldier spirit of courage and self-devotion. In this hymn, as in others, Heber makes much use of the power of a refrain, of which the Psalter gives us so many examples.

(4) "God, that madest earth and heaven" (*Hymns A. & M.* 26). It is seldom that such a short hymn obtains so great a hold. As Heber wrote it, there was only one stanza, and the other was added by Archbishop Whately.

Both stanzas are more or less like an old German morning hymn by Heinrich Albert. The hymn owes much of its popularity to its melodious rhythm, and its tune. Tune will do much for a hymn, a good one or even a bad one, and a dismal, unattractive tune will condemn a fine hymn to never being used. It would be easy to illustrate this from *Hymns A. & M.* This is the worst of that system, otherwise commendable, of printing music with hymns. I do rebel against it as much as I do against the universal "Amen".

(5) There are two others which we must briefly notice, because they are not found in *Hymns A. & M.* The first is an Epiphany hymn, "Brightest and best".

I can hardly believe it was rejected because it is an address to a star. It simply means "may God lead us to our Redeemer, as He led the Magi, by a star". Such criticism is on a level with that which finds fault with "From Greenland's icy mountains" as being chiefly an address to winds and waves.

I am sorry we cannot use it; our Epiphany hymns are not very satisfactory.

Lastly there is "I praised the earth, in beauty seen", a hymn on the transitoriness of the beauties of creation, for the fourth Sunday after Trinity, suggested by the Epistle for that day. It is no doubt florid, as most of Heber's hymns are, but the thought of the last stanza might well ensure it a place in any hymn book.

> O God, O Good beyond compare!
> If thus Thy meaner works are fair,
> If thus Thy bounties gild the span
> Of ruin'd earth and sinful man,
> How glorious must the mansion be
> Where Thy redeem'd shall dwell with Thee!

On the whole, looking back, one can see that the collection, the work of a scholar, a gentleman, and a churchman, would recommend hymns in quarters where hitherto they had been regarded with distaste and dislike, and that without sacrificing spirituality and devotion.

On the other hand, this very refinement, ornament, somewhat florid character, is against their ever gaining a great hold.

The language is often such as would be quite unintelligible to plain working people. There is in these hymns an over-elaboration both of thought and expression—just what we should expect when he writes of "correcting", and perfecting.

Milman. Heber had a colleague, as I have already stated, in Dean Milman, and Heber's florid and elaborate style is surpassed by Milman's. The power and splendour of Milman's descriptions in his *History* are well known. His hymns are of the same character. The best example, perhaps, is the hymn for Palm Sunday, "Ride on! ride on in majesty!" (*Hymns A. & M.* 99). It is a really noble hymn, yet I should be afraid to tell you here what the original third line of the first stanza was; and there are in it expressions like "lowly pomp", and "sapphire throne" which are, to my mind, too rhetorical, too ornate.

There is, however, one hymn of Milman's quite free from these faults, at least in the form in which we use it. It is

> O help us, Lord; each hour of need
>> Thy heavenly succour give. (*Hymns A. & M.* 279)

Here I must pause, on the brink of the great stream of modern hymnody. It is impossible to mention even cursorily any leading names. It is enough to have shown the various sources from which they derived suggestion and inspiration.

I hope I have been able to show that it is worth while studying the hymns we use, as to their authorship, purpose, meaning, and their connexion with the Church Service; and that, by so doing, we make them in their use more profitable, more heartfelt, and so more acceptable to Him to Whom we offer them.

III. THE ATONEMENT[1]

The doctrine of the Atonement has not to-day the prominence that it once had in religion. I will not now attempt an historical survey of the forms it took, and of how it was regarded by the Greek and Latin Fathers. They were various in their presentation of the doctrine, but all were agreed on the essential fact. With regard to early views I will only say that it is not possible to contrast, as is sometimes done, the view of the Greek Fathers as a whole with the Latin, for Irenaeus and Origen, Athanasius and Chrysostom, cannot be classed together; they represent different views though not mutually exclusive ones.

The Latin Fathers, however, Hilary, Ambrose, Augustine, and Gregory, emphasise more strongly than the Greeks the transcendent importance for the salvation of man which is to be attributed to the Cross. Anselm follows, centuries afterwards, in the track of Augustine. I shall hope to say something later of his great work, *Cur Deus Homo?* He contrasts the various subjective theories of the Atonement which allow it no other significance and effect than that which it has upon *us* and *our* affections, and *our* will, with the objective view which regards it as offered on our behalf to God.

The Reformation opened new questions, though both sides in that great controversy held firmly to the

[1] Salisbury Cathedral, Advent, 1916.

objective character of the atoning work of Christ; that is to say, that a real atonement was accomplished on the cross, and not merely suffering endured which was intended to affect us by the revelation of Divine love. When we grieve over the deep rift which divides the Western Church, we can remember with thankfulness that, as to the atoning work of Christ on the cross, we are of one faith with our Roman brethren, who hold firmly the objective view. We are united at present in that matter and shall so remain one with them, as long as we continue in the faith grounded and settled. But there are currents of thought to-day which tend to undermine this faith, and that is why I want to bring this subject before you.

There is an indifference as to this doctrine which is a real danger. I have said that there is less interest in it than in earlier times, or even in the times of our fathers, and this is strange, for the definite characteristic of Anglican religion to-day is the greater value of the Sacrament of the Holy Communion. What is that service? It is a commemoration of the death of Christ and of the benefits which we receive thereby. We cannot discern its significance without a clear conviction of the objective value of the death of Christ, as that which took away sin and obtained its forgiveness. Yet, again, there has been in our own day a greatly increased observance of Good Friday, and indeed of Holy Week, though this is true only of attached Church members, and not of professing Christians generally. Does this point to an adequate sense of the significance of the Cross? It seems to me that there is a danger of sentimentalism. Preachers dwell with pathos on the sufferings of Christ and use every effort to evoke sympathy. Of this Faber's hymn is the type: "O come and mourn with me awhile". That is not what the Cross should awaken—not sympathy with a sufferer, but awe and adoration, unspeakable thankfulness for a mighty mystery of salvation.

The reasons why the fact of the Atonement is losing its hold over the conscience of English churchmen appear to me to be three:

I. The disposition to merge the fact of the death of Christ in the wider fact of the Incarnation.

II. A reaction against exaggerated and unguarded statements of the doctrine of an objective atonement.

III. A failing sense of sin and guilt and judgment to come, of sin as calling for atonement.

I will speak of each of these separately.

I. The Church owes much to Bishop Westcott and other writers of the last generation for their development of the significance of the Incarnation. In the Incarnation Bishop Westcott taught us to see the revelation of personal, social, and national duties. The fullest statement of his thought on the subject is, I think, a course of sermons he preached in Westminster Abbey, and published in the latter half of the volume entitled *Christus Consummator*. There, in a sermon on the Incarnation and the Fall, after emphasising the unity of mankind and its solidarity, the restorative power which love can exercise upon it, he goes on to say that the measure of love's restorative efficacy lies in knowledge and sympathy and holiness. Let the knowledge be complete; let the sympathy reach to every creature; let the holiness be absolute, and *there* is provision for the atonement of fallen humanity. In short, it is the Incarnation, including all that Christ was, did, said, and suffered which is the Atonement. The death on the cross is only one element among others in its efficacy.

Now, there can be no doubt that the elucidation of all that is contained in the Incarnation of the Son of God has been very fruitful in our time, and especially in the direction in which Bishop Westcott desired it should be, in recognition of our social duties. But this movement of thought has tended to obscure the *primary* place of the death of Christ in our conception of His work, to obscure it in a way which does not respond with its treatment in Scripture. Reflect, first, on the attitude of the Lord Himself. This has been well emphasised by Dr Dale in his Second Lecture on *The Atonement*, 13th ed., pp. 52–4. Then, even if you confine your view to St Mark, there are His three prophecies of His death;[1] and consider the fulness with which the incidents of the Passion are given in all the four Gospels. Moreover, it is in St Mark, the earliest and most original of the three Synoptists, that the emphasis on the Passion is greatest. Notice in St Mark the disproportion between the Passion and the rest of the narrative. "The narrative of the

[1] Mark viii. 31, ix. 31, x. 34.

Passion is on a scale out of all proportion to that on which the ministry is drawn."[1]

It would be natural to go on and show the place and function assigned to the Cross apart from the Incarnation in the salvation of mankind as they appear in the Epistles of St Paul, St Peter, and St John; but I propose to take all this evidence later when we come to the various aspects of the Passion as a Sacrifice, a Reconciliation, and a Ransom.

II. The second cause which accounts for the obscuration of the objective view of the Atonement is the reaction against exaggerated and misleading statements of it. One element in them which rightly awakened opposition was the suggested contrast between the Persons of the Blessed Trinity, the wrath of the Father, and the compassion of the Son. Such distinction of the attributes of the Father and the Son is contrary to all that we know and believe regarding the Blessed Trinity. The preachers of the Atonement had not clearly recognised that the offering was the *Father's* offering, no less than that of the Son. "God sent His Son" is the constant phrase of Scripture— and perhaps such words are not even now sufficiently emphasised. "God was in Christ reconciling the world to Himself."

III. But there is a more fundamental reason for the indifference with which the doctrine of the Atonement is regarded, and the complaisance with which ex-

[1] Swete, *Gospel according to St Mark*, p. lv.

planations of it are received, explanations which dissolve its objective character, and make the Cross of Christ little more than an example of obedience or an appeal to human affections. The reason is that the want of atonement is *not felt*, and that the moral standard of to-day is relaxed till there is in many quarters little sense of guilt entailing judgment. The idea of punishment as *retribution* is being gradually dismissed from the place it held as between man and man. It is said that punishment is only reformatory or preventive, consequently it is supposed that we may dismiss retributive punishment from our conception of the action of God.

But, reason as you will, you cannot silence the conscience of the sinner on the one hand, which confesses that punishment is deserved, nor can you silence righteous indignation on the other, which cries out for some just penalty on the guilty. Not long ago there was a wave of national feeling which reasserted the old retributive view, which required that those who had done cruel and shameful things in the war should meet with some just recompense. It is not a question of *reprisals*, which is a different matter, but of public vindication of moral law. Reprisals and retaliation are plainly forbidden in Scripture.

This, however, is by the way. I only want to protest against the theory that retributive punishment can have no place in human or Divine dealing with the sinner. It has a place in both. However, our sense of the need of atonement is *personal*, arising not from the sins which we see in others, but from those which we are conscious of in ourselves. And it is because the consciousness of sin is deficient in England to-day, especially in the educated classes, that the Gospel of the Atonement has been explained away without calling out a protest, or has been changed into something else, which may satisfy sentimental religion, but cannot really meet the needs of a burdened soul.

All this has been prefatory. Now let us come close to our subject.

I must begin by saying that we are dealing with a *mystery* to the essence of which we cannot pierce. We can, I believe, clear our conceptions, discard mistakes, and learn to feel more deeply and practically certain aspects of the Cross—but when all has been said we shall acknowledge that there is more which we cannot explain, although we know it is there by the testimony of experience. Let us, then, approach it with reverence and with awe.

Secondly, no single aspect of the Cross is comprehensive of itself or exclusive of others. We shall find that the Cross radiates power on many sides in many ways. A Divine act—much more, the greatest of Divine acts—has many purposes to fulfil, and our present endeavour will be rather to enumerate and dwell upon these, than to attempt to combine them in any *one* theory.

We will start from a single text contained in that solemn statement of the essentials of St Paul's preaching which he gives to meet all the doubts of the Corinthian Church, "Christ died for our sins" (I. Cor. xv. 3).

I am speaking to those who would recognise Divine

inspiration in *all* St Paul's written words, but this short clause has a special attestation. He says it is what he received and delivered to them even as he had received it. I do not think I need stay to prove that this means a special Divine revelation made to him, as was the case also with regard to his account of the institution of the Lord's Supper in the same Epistle. It does *not* mean that he had received it from the Twelve, or any other human source. Compare Gal. i. 12, where he says of the Gospel which he preached: "I received it not from man, nor was taught it, but received it by revelation from Jesus Christ".

Let us now return to the words, "Christ died for our sins". This is a statement of the purpose and object of His death, and it is also a statement as to which part of His manifestation on earth was in closest relation to our sins. Each is linked as closely as possible to the other, His death and our sins. The added words, "according to the scriptures", are, mainly at least, a reference to the prophecy of the Servant of the Lord in Is. liii.

We have now to consider what light the New Testament as a whole gives on the words of the text. We shall find, I think, that it may be best considered under four heads.

The death of Christ was (1) a Sacrifice, (2) a Reconciliation, (3) a Ransom, (4) a Punishment or Penalty. There are other aspects on which I will touch later, but these are the principal. You will notice at once that I do not give the word "Atonement" as one of these heads, and I will now explain why I do not.

"Atonement" is a convenient word to express the doctrine as a whole, but there is an etymological difficulty about employing it, when we come to a closer analysis of Scripture teaching. By its *derivation* the word means *one* thing; by its theological and its popular use it means *another*. To atone is to make at-one, i.e. to bring together persons or things who have in some measure been *separated*. So, in Shakespeare's *Othello*, Desdemona says, in reply to the question, "Is there division between my lord and Cassio"? "I would do much to atone them".[1] No idea of expiation here, only to bring together Othello and Cassio. In short, it is plain that the original meaning of the word was *reconciliation*. This is the sense in which our translators employed it. Rom. v. 11, "By Whom we have now received the atonement" ("reconciliation" in Revised Version). The Greek word καταλλαγή is translated accurately in II. Cor. v. 18, 19, "the ministry of reconciliation", and "the word of reconciliation". So, you see, Atonement will come under Reconciliation in our consideration of the passage in Romans quoted above, which is the only occurrence of the word "atonement" in the Authorised Version of the New Testament.

But the case is different with regard to very numerous passages of the Old Testament in which "atonement", or "making atonement", occurs. There, "to make an atonement" is the translation of a Hebrew word

[1] *Othello*, IV. i. 244.

which has nothing of the sense of reconciliation. It is a verb which means *to cover sin* in the sense of taking away its guilt, or expiating it, neutralising its effects and obliterating it. The Great Day of Atonement would be better rendered as the Day of *Expiation*. It is from this use of the word "atone" in our translation of the Hebrew *kipper* in the Old Testament, that the word "atonement" has imbibed the sense of *expiation* which it now has in common language, instead of its original sense of *reconciliation*. Atonement in this modern sense will therefore have to be considered as expiation under the head of Sacrifice; and Atonement in the ancient sense of the word under the head of Reconciliation. Propitiation (Rom. iii. 25) will also come under the head of Sacrifice.

All these three aspects of the Cross belong to the objective view of atonement, namely, that something was done upon the cross which had effects besides and beyond those other which it has had ever since on souls to whom the story came. The subjective view is no doubt of the highest importance, has abundant evidence in Scripture, and has been fully set forth in our own time. But alone it is *not adequate* to embrace the whole teaching of Scripture, and it is to Scripture, not to philosophy, that we must go for explanation. That is what I hope to show you as we consider the three aspects I have already mentioned, Sacrifice, Reconciliation, and Ransom, in the passages in which they occur.

LECTURE II

I. *Sacrifice*

The Apostles regard the death of Christ on the cross as a *Sacrifice*, and they connect it with the sacrificial system of the Old Covenant. It is not merely that from their education they so regard it, but they were, I believe, directed so to regard it by the Spirit. We must remember that the Hebrew sacrificial system does not stand alone. It is part of a universal conception prevalent in all nations from the earliest times that sacrifice is the necessary way of approaching the Divinity. Is this conception a pitiable mistake, or may we recognise in its universality a true instinct preparatory for the explanation and confirmation which it received in the Sacrifice of the Son of God?

The words of Rev. xiii. 8, "The Lamb slain *from the foundation of the world*", confirm what we gather elsewhere as to the eternal purpose of God, that Christ should die as a Sacrifice. Surely the instinct of sacrifice was a presentiment and silent prophecy of what was to come in the fulness of time? The universal instinct of mankind received a definite and manifold development in the institutions of the Hebrew nation. And on the eve of the great event our Lord Himself spoke the words which were to link the type and antitype, the blood shed to ratify the Old Covenant (Ex. xxiv. 8) and the blood shed as the condition and seal of the New Covenant: "This cup is the new covenant in My blood" (Luke xxii. 20).

Not only this, but the Sacrifice on the cross is also

linked with that of the Paschal Lamb by being contemporary with the Passover. It is also linked with the sin-offering and the guilt-offering by our Lord's own words, "My blood which is poured out for you" (Luke xxii. 20), and to this He adds in St Matthew a more definite statement of the purpose: "which is shed for many unto remission of sins" (Matt. xxvi. 28). The thought of Christ as the antitype of the Paschal Lamb is taken up most fully in the Apocalypse, where He is spoken of under that title no less than twenty-nine times.

Let us proceed to consider the passages in the Epistles in which the writers develop the thought of the *Sacrifice* of the cross. I shall quote from the Revised Version.

I. Cor. v. 7: "Our Passover also hath been sacrificed, even Christ".

Eph. v. 2: "Even as Christ gave Himself up for us, an offering and a sacrifice to God".

It is hardly necessary to quote from the Epistle to the Hebrews. The *whole* Epistle is instinct with the idea of Christ's sacrifice of Himself, as replacing and fulfilling the sacrifices of the Old Dispensation, and particularly the writer connects the sacrifice of Christ with that which the High Priest offered on the Day of Atonement. Those who assign to the death of Christ a purely subjective value do practically set aside the Epistle to the Hebrews as fanciful and misleading. The only sacrifice which they acknowledge is a sacrifice in the thin figurative sense which the word now has, an unselfish giving up of something, whether it be of life or only of some personal advantage. This is *not* what St Paul meant when he said Christ was sacrificed, or gave Himself as a sacrifice. Such a figurative conception is thoroughly excluded by the emphasis on *blood* in the Epistles of St Paul, St Peter, and St John in the Apocalypse, and most of all in the Epistle to the Hebrews.

Rom. v. 9: "Being now justified by His *blood*".

Eph. ii. 13: "Ye...are made nigh in the *blood* of Christ".

Col. i. 20: "Having made peace through the *blood* of His Cross".

I. Pet. i. 2: "Unto obedience and sprinkling of the *blood* of Jesus Christ".

I. John i. 7: "The *blood* of Jesus His Son cleanseth us from all sin".

Rev. i. 5: "Unto Him that loosed us from our sins by His *blood*".

As to the Epistle to the Hebrews, it is, as I said before, superfluous to quote special passages as to the effect of the sacred blood. It must, however, be observed in that Epistle that the death and the blood are also regarded in the light of necessary ratification of a new covenant. A covenant, especially an eternal covenant, needs death and blood for its ratification.

The interpretation urged by Bishop Westcott and others is, that in the New Testament blood always represents the life which can be available for use only when liberated by death, and therefore it may be inferred that the passages quoted do not involve a strictly sacrificial view. It is indeed true that Christ died to impart to us life, His life, but I cannot think that these passages are susceptible of nothing more than such an interpretation. They point to a sacrificial death of which the shedding of blood is the symbol, and not to the bestowal of life.

If, then, the Apostolic teaching concerning the death of Christ presents it as a sacrifice offered to God, we next inquire the *purpose* of the sacrifice. Here we are met by an important word, "propitiation". "To propitiate" means *to make favourable*, and is applicable to persons, not to things. If we speak of propitiation, we feel at once that there is a danger of regarding God as angry and needing to be appeased. There is indeed a wrath of God, or at least an attitude of the Divine Mind so represented, but we are on the edge of heathen conceptions of Deity. It will be necessary, therefore, to examine the passages in which the word occurs, and its Hebrew and Greek originals.

Let us take, first, the two familiar passages in I. John ii. 2 and iv. 10. Our rendering "propitiation" is taken from the Vulgate. Let me quote a passage from Dr A. E. Brooke's note on the first of these passages in his *Commentary on the Johannine Epistles*: "The object of propitiation in Jewish thought, as shown in their Scriptures, is (1) not God (as in Greek thought), but *man*, who has estranged himself from God, or (2) the *sins* which have intervened between him and his God. They must be *covered* before right relations can be restored between God and His worshippers".[1] That word *covered* is the important word.

[1] *Op. cit.* p. 28.

In explaining the words "atone" and "atonement", as occurring in our version of the Old Testament, I said that they were used to represent the Hebrew כִּפֶּר (*kipper*) of which the radical meaning is *to cover*. It is applied in the Old Testament to the ritual of the Day of Atonement, and to the effect of the whole system of sin, trespass, and guilt offering. These were the appointed ways of *covering* sin. Now the LXX usually renders this word "cover" by a Greek verb ἱλάσκομαι, which is cognate to the word ἱλασμός, which we have in these passages of St John, and we may therefore interpret the word used by St John by the usage of the Hebrew כִּפֶּר (*kipper*). This shows us that the scriptural conception of ἱλασμός is not, as it appeared to be, *propitiation*, applied to appease one who is angry, namely, God, but a means of altering the character of sin and the standing of the sinner. As regards the sin, it is better expressed as *expiation* rather than propitiation, though of course our familiarity with these two important texts has led to a half-conscious modification of the meaning of propitiation. The other passage where "propitiation" occurs is in Romans iii. 25, where the Greek word is slightly different, though cognate. It is the word which in the LXX and in Heb. ix. 5 stands for the *mercy-seat*, on which the blood was sprinkled on the Day of Atonement. The Hebrew name of the mercy-seat, כַּפֹּרֶת (*kapporeth*), signified literally a covering placed over the ark, but the use made of that covering on the Day of Atonement, namely, for sprinkling of blood, led to its being translated in the LXX by a word which did *not* mean a covering in a literal sense, but in a spiritual sense a place or means for covering sin, namely, ἱλαστήριον. But in Rom. iii. 25 I think ἱλαστήριον is rightly translated "to be a propitiation", not "as a mercy-seat".

The practical result is that where we say that the death of Christ on the cross was propitiatory, we mean that it covered human sin, or expiated it, and so brought the sinner into right relation with God, not that it appeased the anger of God. Whether any change in God's attitude to us was effected will come under the head of Reconciliation, not of Propitiation.

Lastly, as against any unworthy conception of an angry God needing to be appeased, we must remember that the sacrifice was God's *own* sacrifice. He sent His Son to be a Sacrifice, and God was in Christ, in whose person the Sacrifice was made. In the Sacrifice of the Cross *God* covered sin. The Atonement, if I may use the word in its widest sense, was made not to God, but by God. In short, the Sacrifice was not propitiatory in the usual sense, but *expiatory*. An expiation was needed if God was to forgive sin. This does not mean that God was fettered by a law higher than Himself requiring expiation as a condition of forgiveness. He Himself is that law.

I will now quote a passage from Dr Dale, *The Atonement*, Lecture IX: "Our own conscience testifies to the fact that sin deserves punishment. There is an eternal law of righteousness, according to which we feel ourselves deserving of punishment, unless by transgression we have blunted and deadened conscience. God has revealed Himself to us, and we recognise in a *living Person* the same august and supreme authority which conscience confessed in the eternal law of Righteousness. If God does not assert the principle that sin deserves punishment by *actually* punishing it, He must assert the principle some other way. Some divine act is required which shall have all the moral worth and significance of the act by which the penalties of sin would have been inflicted on the sinner". Read the whole of Lecture IX. It is true that such considerations are but guesses at Divine mysteries, in which we are liable to lose our footing, but they have the merit of corresponding both with deep human instincts and with passages of Scripture, the lead of which they seek to follow instead of explaining them away.

You will see that what I said above about the really retributive nature of punishment lies at the basis of Dr Dale's argument.

II. *Reconciliation*

The second aspect in which Scripture presents the death of Christ is as effecting *reconciliation*. The passages in which reconciliation is spoken of are all in Epistles of St Paul. It is a Pauline aspect of the Cross —it is the consequence of the sacrifice, that is to say, of the expiation. First the sacrifice, then reconciliation. You may remember I said before that the English word which is used to cover all the aspects of the doctrine, namely, *atonement*, is really, so far as its original meaning goes, equivalent to reconciliation, and hence in one passage (namely, Rom. v. 11) we find "atonement" in the Authorised Version, where the words in the original (τὴν καταλλαγήν) ought, as elsewhere, to have been translated "the reconciliation". When that correction has been made, as is the case in the Revised Version, the word "atonement" disappears altogether from the New Testament. After what I have already said as to the aspect of Christ's death as an expiation, you will see that the absence from Scripture of the familiar word has no bearing whatever on the objective character of what we are in the habit of calling the Doctrine of the Atonement. One other remark is necessary as to the use of the words "reconcile" and "reconciliation". They occur also in the Old Testament, but there they represent the Hebrew word, or family of words, which we considered above under the head of "propitiation" or covering of sin. For instance, they are applied to the ritual cleansing of the Sanctuary by Aaron on the Day of Atonement: Lev. xvi. 20, A.V.: "When he hath made an end of *reconciling* the holy place", i.e. of purging it from the involuntary uncleanness of priests and people. From this use of the word "reconcile" has come its application to the ceremonial practised when a church has been profaned by murder or other evil deed committed in it. It is, of course, obvious that such uses of the word "reconcile" are quite different from its significance in the Epistles of St Paul. There it is a reconciliation of *persons*—of God and man. A reconciliation between *men* implies a mutual responsive change of attitude in both parties. Is this the case in the reconciliation which was brought about by the Cross? The second of the Thirty-nine Articles describes the purpose of Christ's Passion; it was "to *reconcile* the Father to us". It has been maintained that the change effected can only be a change in *us*, a change from the enmity of disobedience and unbelief, and not a change in the attitude of *God* towards us. This change in *us* was, it is said, all that the Cross effected, that is to say, its effect was purely *subjective*, and on us. But there is a frequent mention of the anger of God as directed against sinners, as for instance Rom. ii. 5–9. When that anger ceases to be so directed, there is surely a change (or what we should be compelled to call a change) on the part of God as well as on the part of man.[1] Sin is guilt, guilt deserves punishment. Punishment cannot be dispensed with unless the guilt be expiated. Without expiation of guilt there could be no remission of sin. In his book, *The Work of Christ*, Dr Forsyth says, "God could will nothing against His holy and righteous nature, and the judgment which is bound up with it against sin", and perhaps he is right in suggesting that the change implied in reconciliation is a change in God's *view and treatment* of the sinful world, rather than a change in His affection as Creator for the work of His hands. Dr Forsyth also rightly emphasises the thought that the reconciliation made by the Cross is primarily a reconciliation between God and mankind *as a whole*.

[1] Sanday and Headlam, *Commentary on the Epistle to the Romans*, p. 130.

I must deprecate the purely subjective view of reconciliation by the Cross, as though its effect was only manward and not Godward. Yet it is most true that it is under this aspect that the effect of the Cross has been powerful and availing. So our Lord Himself regarded it when He said, "I, if I be lifted up from the earth, will draw all men unto Me" (John xii. 32). The Godward effect of the Cross is a mystery at which we can only guess, but the manward effect is a matter of the widest and most varied human experience. On that subjective effect I shall dwell in the next lecture, and, while showing its importance, I shall also endeavour to show its inadequacy when regarded as the whole explanation of the Cross. Here I will add that there is something peculiarly touching and comforting in the thought of reconciliation. Some of the happiest moments in human life have been moments of reconciliation between hearts long estranged. Still happier is the moment when a sinner feels himself again, or for the first time, at peace with God. This is what filled St Paul's heart with joy. It was the consciousness that to him had been entrusted the ministry of *reconciliation*. It is a great thing to be a peacemaker between man and man, a greater to be a peacemaker between man and God.

Before leaving the subject, we must also notice a passage in which reconciliation takes a wider sweep, and includes, not mankind only, but all creation (Col. i. 19, 20): "It was the good pleasure of the Father through Him [i.e. Christ] to reconcile all things unto Himself, having made peace through the blood of His

Cross; through Him, I say, whether things upon the earth, or things in the heavens". Does not the Apostle hint that Christ's redemption, accomplished here, spread its effects to other worlds than ours? Then he goes on to speak of the Colossians, to whom he writes as included in this universal reconciliation. And it is a reconciliation which the Father has been pleased to make by the blood of the Cross, by the death of the Son, not merely by His incarnation. There is also in the Epistle to the Ephesians a supplementary thought that the universal reconciliation of believers to the Father contains and involves the reconciliation of Jew and Gentile (Eph. ii. 16).

III. *Ransom, or Redemption*

As a matter of etymology these two words are one. "Ransom" is a shortened form of the Latin *redemptionem*. But they have acquired distinct associations. Ransom is specially a consideration or price given for the deliverance of a prisoner of war. But the original word of which "ransom" is an abbreviation was derived from *redimo*, "to buy back", and means any deliverance or recovery of a person or property which has been alienated. Further, the meaning of "redemption" expanded so as to connote any deliverance in the widest sense without implying that a price is paid for it.

The supreme interest of this aspect of the death of Christ is that it was thus He Himself chose to describe it to His disciples, "The Son of man came to give His life a ransom for many" (Mark x. 45, and Matt. xx. 28).

The word used by our Lord must have been the Hebrew *kopher* (or its Aramaic equivalent), which is frequent in the Old Testament, e.g. "None of them can by any means redeem his brother, nor give to God a ransom for him" (Ps. xlix. 7), i.e. a ransom to deliver him from dying, or from the power of Death personified. Is it possible to fix with exactness the sense in which our Lord used the word? We find it in Num. xxxv. 31 used of ransom for a life which has been forfeited by crime: "Ye shall take no ransom for the life of a manslayer, which is guilty of death: but he shall surely be put to death". It would seem there to be ransom for those who would otherwise suffer for their crimes. And the ransom is on the principle of a life given for a life forfeited.

There are, however, other associations with the idea of ransom and redemption, which in a secondary way would be suggested by the word used by Christ, and still more by the passages in which His saying is developed in the Epistles of St Paul and the Epistle to the Hebrews. Redemption of alienated property had its place in Hebrew law, and so had the redemption of a slave. The deliverance of Israel from Egypt was regarded as a redemption or recovery by God of the nation which was His property, and at the same time as the deliverance of the nation from its slavery under Pharaoh. This great double redemption was a type of the still greater deliverance which God effected in Christ, by which He recovered us from the dominion of sin and death, gave us our freedom, and regained us for Himself. This is what is meant by Christ's title,

"Our Redeemer". Possibly in common usage the larger connotation of that title is often overlooked.

There are further thoughts which should always be connected with Redemption. It is a recovery by God of what is truly His. We have fallen under the dominion of another lord. Now God has regained His own. Secondly, our recovery for God has been bought at a price: "Ye are not your own; for ye were bought with a price" (I. Cor. vi. 20. Compare also I. Pet. i. 18, 19, Rev. v. 9, A.V.).

There is yet another suggestion, more distantly connected with redemption, but part of the idea of it in Hebrew law, and deeply symbolical. Redemption of alienated property and vindication of the oppressed, were both the privilege and duty of the nearest kinsman, the Goël. This word is translated in A.V. sometimes the "avenger" (so in Pentateuch), sometimes the "kinsman" (so in Ruth), elsewhere the "redeemer" (so in Psalms and Isaiah). Therefore the Son of God became our kinsman, that He might have the right to be our Redeemer, and to obtain for us an "eternal redemption" (Heb. ix. 12).

Out of this true and profound aspect of the Passion arose a strange and profane inference which for centuries held its place in theology. It was supposed that, if there was a ransom, it must have had a recipient. The recipient must have been Satan, as it was in his power that the Saviour found the world. Satan had rights over us which were recognised by the ransom which was paid him in the death of Christ. This view was current in the Church, along with other and sounder views of the Atonement, until the great work of Anselm, *Cur Deus Homo?* gave it its death-blow and replaced it by something better, the doctrine of the Cross as a satisfaction, which with modifications may be regarded as holding its ground to-day. That view, as I say, needs modifications. Anselm, imbued with the feudal conceptions of his age, thought of God too much as a feudal lord whose honour had been compromised, and to whom therefore satisfaction was due. Still, the word used did in some way approach the truth, and with due reserve was retained in Western theology generally, and in particular in our own Articles and Prayer Book: "Who made there a full, perfect, and sufficient sacrifice, oblation, and satisfaction" (*Prayer of Consecration*).

As I am not now attempting to deal with the history of the doctrine, I will say no more on Anselm's position. It is enough to have noticed one of the errors which may arise from a too literal interpretation, and too precise inferences drawn from the figurative expressions by which Scripture has revealed to us the meaning and virtue of the Cross.

We have considered the three principal aspects in which Scripture presents the death of Christ. Is there yet another? Was it penal? For the three already dealt with we have definite New Testament words, θυσία (sacrifice), καταλλαγή (reconciliation), λύτρον (ransom), with the verbs which correspond to these substantives. It is not so in the case of the penal aspect of the Cross. Yet there are passages which seem to imply it very distinctly, especially I. Pet. ii. 21–25. That

THE ATONEMENT

passage is, of course, based on Is. liii, so it is necessary
to go back to that. It is clear that the whole prophecy
of the Servant of Jehovah, of which Is. liii is a part,
was understood as applying to Christ by the Apostles,
who four times speak of Him by this name in Acts iii
and iv, though the reference is hidden by the mis-
translation "child" instead of "servant". Not only so,
but our Lord Himself claims the Isaianic prophecy as
referring to Himself (Luke xxii. 37). We must, however, not quote the parallel passage in Mark xv. 28, as
it has not sufficient documentary authority. It has
been implied or stated by recent critics that the objective view of the effects of the death of Christ grew out
of a misunderstanding of Is. liii. If it was a misunderstanding, it was shared by Christ Himself. It is
true that the prophecy of the Servant, spread over
several passages in Is. xli to liii inclusive, fluctuates
between three conceptions: (1) Israel as a whole,
(2) the chosen remnant of Israel, (3) "an individual
figure in whom all the attributes of the Servant cul-
minate". It is this last interpretation which alone can
satisfy the language of lii. 13–liii. 12. "It is impossible
for us who read this passage in the light of its fulfilment
to doubt that it was intended by the Holy Spirit to
point forward to Christ."[1] We have, therefore, to
consider the testimony of Is. liii. Here there is, first,
the sacrificial view. In liii. 10 the Servant's life is to be
a guilt-offering (Heb. *asham*). But the greatly pre-
ponderant view of the death is that of a punishment,
as in verse 5, "The chastisement [punishment] of our

[1] Kirkpatrick, *Doctrine of the Prophets*, Lecture XIII.

202

peace [leading to peace for us] was upon Him"; and verse 6, "The Lord hath laid on Him the iniquity of us all"; verse 11, "He shall bear their iniquities"; verse 12, "He bare the sin of many". These last expressions are taken up by St Peter (I. Pet. ii. 24), "Who His own self bare our sins in His body upon the tree". If we ask what is meant by bearing sins, we find that throughout the Old Testament it means bearing the punishment due to sin. Lam. v. 7 may stand as one instance out of many: "Our fathers have sinned, and are not; and we have borne their iniquities". Two Hebrew verbs are used to express this bearing of sins, both with the same sense. The same view of Christ's sufferings appears again in I. Pet. iii. 18, "Christ also hath once suffered for sins". Sacrifice and punishment are quite distinct conceptions. It is the latter of the two which St Peter here presents to us. We shall next have to consider whether these two aspects of the Cross, sacrifice and punishment, are compatible or mutually exclusive.

LECTURE III

IV. *Punishment*

In the preceding lecture I attempted with some hesitation to show that there was a fourth aspect in which the death of Christ should be regarded, namely, as a penalty, punishment, or judgment. The passages there considered imply that Christ did in some way take upon Himself the sin of the world, and in consequence bore the punishment due to the sin of the world. It

THE ATONEMENT

was not simply a taking away or removing of sin (an explanation which might suffice for John i. 29, "The Lamb of God, which taketh away the sin of the world", or I. John iii. 5), but an actual bearing of it as laid on Him. The Greek words in the two passages just quoted, ὁ αἴρων, are also susceptible of the latter interpretation as well as the former, and the R.V. margin in both places gives, as an alternative, "bear" instead of "take away". It is true that there seems to be an incompatibility between a sacrifice which averts punishment, and an actual endurance of punishment. Can the same event have both characters? We can reply that both are combined in the prophecy of Is. liii. And there the victim offered in the sacrifice is also the sin-bearer who endures the punishment.

Does this view of the Cross as punishment imply that vicarious character of the Cross of Christ as a substitution for punishment on us, which has not unnaturally given offence to many minds? It is certainly asserted by St Peter that He suffered for sins, the just on behalf (ὑπέρ) of the unjust (I. Pet. iii. 18). But I do not think these words mean substitution. We must consider who and what Christ was. He was not a man who after His birth was made God, but a Divine Person who assumed humanity for a special purpose, namely, that He might take on Himself its debt of guilt, and pay it once for all. Had He been an ordinary man in whom the Spirit of God dwelt in some special way, then the selection by God of such a man for punishment instead of other men would have been inconceivable. But the difficulty does not apply with the same force to a Divine Person who voluntarily assumed human nature with all its inseparable collective liabilities. To reinforce this conception of the assumption of the sin of mankind by the Son of God as attached to His human nature, we have the phenomena of the Agony and the Passion. It is, I venture to think, quite possible to regard the Agony as produced by intense realisation of the coming physical torture, and so Jeremy Taylor appears to consider it in a well-known passage on the Fear of Death.[1] But it is more usual to regard it as also the result of the close contact of a sinless nature with the horror of the world's sin then undertaken by Him.

The cry from the cross, "Eli, Eli, lama sabachthani?", seems to go further still in support of the view that punishment was being endured, and that a part of it was the hiding of the Father's face, and interruption of communion with Him. It is certainly very difficult to reconcile this view, so commonly held, with the full doctrine of the Incarnation, the one Person, and the two Natures, but yet not more difficult than other problems of the Incarnation. If the Cross is to be regarded in a penal light, such an effect would seem to be almost inevitable. On the other hand, "Eli, Eli", may be regarded, not in the light of the opening words alone, but as revealing to us that the whole of the Psalm which they introduce (Ps. xxii) was in the Saviour's mind as the prophecy and pattern of the sufferings which He had willed to endure. So I prefer to leave undecided this difficult question of the penal

[1] *Holy Dying*, Chap. III. 8 (6).

aspect of the Cross, though I do so with the conviction that it has to be considered, and is founded on Scripture. I would rather let the undoubted aspects of (1) Sacrifice, (2) Reconciliation, and (3) Ransom stand as sufficiently representative, to our limited understanding, of the objective value of the Death of Christ, as distinguished from its effects on man, and yet at the same time intimately united with those effects and dependent on them for its saving application to the individual soul.

It is the relation of the individual soul to the Atonement, made once for all, that we must next consider. For to represent the Atonement as a transaction which we simply believe in as a fact, and thereby obtain salvation, is in effect a perversion of the doctrine, though it may seem on the surface to be consistent with the language of Scripture. "Belief" is a large word, and contains much more than intellectual assent. There is, indeed, an element in the Atonement in which we have no part. It has been made for us; this we must maintain. But, as there is a response on the part of God to the offering of the Son, so on our part there is an indispensable response to the appeal which the offering makes, an association of ourselves with all that it implies, a response to its condemnation of sin, a movement on our part toward the mutual reconciliation which it effected, an assertion in our action of the spiritual deliverance and freedom which were obtained by the ransom of the precious blood. This evoking of a response from us is the subjective efficacy of the precious blood, on which so far I have hardly touched. It is this which moralises, so to speak, the doctrine of the Atonement, and gives ethical significance to that which otherwise would be only a partial revelation of a Divine mystery. Christ, as St Peter says, suffered for us "that He might bring us to God" (I. Pet. iii. 18). The way to God has been opened, but that does not avail unless each one of us traverses it, in company indeed with our brethren, but at the same time with the definite effort of the individual soul. So all the objective values of the Cross as Sacrifice, Reconciliation, and Ransom are in a measure realisable by us also in our personal relation to the Father. There is no room for the charge of externalism or disjunction of the human soul from the Atonement on which it relies, a charge which is sometimes made against those who maintain its objective character.

The anxiety of thoughtful Christians to repudiate an unmoral doctrine of the Atonement has led to various modes of treatment of its subjective side, and in some cases to an entire obscuration of its Godward effect. Such is the case in Canon Wilson's Hulsean Lectures, which, owing to their depth of feeling and beauty of expression, have obtained a wide circulation, and probably considerable influence. For all, or nearly all, that he says of the power of the Cross on the human soul, and its fitness to move, raise, and guide us, I have nothing but admiration and sympathy. But he deliberately refuses to admit anything beyond this. You will see the gulf between his view and that which I have attempted to emphasise, in the way in which he deals with the scriptural phrases describing Christ's death as Sacrifice, Expiation, and Ransom. Of these he says, "To abandon these words is impossible, to retain and purge them from the error they connote is the task before us".[1]

I will now ask your attention to a quite different treatment of the subject. Twenty years ago the late Dr Robert Moberly published a book entitled *Atonement and Personality*. His critics unanimously acknowledged it as a work of great ability and importance. It was warmly welcomed by many readers as apparently retaining the Catholic doctrine of an objective Atonement, while endeavouring to meet the difficulties involved in that doctrine by a comparatively new presentation of the efficacy of the Cross both towards God and towards man. He represented the Atonement as made, not by vicarious punishment endured, but by vicarious penitence consummated in the Cross. The line of thought is as follows. He recognises that the question of the nature of punishment lies at the foundation of all treatment of the doctrine. His first chapter is on Punishment, and he definitely gives up its retributive character. Punishment, whether by God or man, is corrective and restorative. If it ever becomes retributive (which he concedes it does), it is only when all its efforts have failed, and in the case of the permanently impenitent. The whole purpose of punishment is answered by its development of penitence in the sufferer. What man needs is, therefore, perfect penitence, which makes

[1] *How Christ saves Us*, Lecture II.

forgiveness possible. The chapter on Forgiveness is most interesting and valuable. Next we come to a puzzling paradox. Perfect penitence is only possible for a sinless being who has had no experience of sin. The atoning work of Christ on behalf of man was His perfect penitence for the sins of the whole world. This penitence of Christ by the gift of the Spirit becomes ours, is accepted for us, obtains our full forgiveness, restores us to righteousness and communion with God.

I do not pretend that it is possible in such brief sentences to do justice to a great book, subtle in thought and somewhat difficult in language. But this summary is sufficient to show the points which I think have been justly criticised.

1. The abandonment of the retributive nature of punishment as its primary character. This character of punishment lies at the basis of the whole discussion. It is crucial for deciding on the objective element in the Atonement. Does sin deserve punishment, or merely call for correction and reformation by pain or otherwise? If it does not deserve punishment, then there is no law of eternal righteousness needing vindication. In support of the conviction that sin deserves punishment, I would appeal again to the general instinct of mankind, as apart from and untouched by philosophical arguments. It has been truly said by one who is himself a philosopher that "punishment is that which the sinner's own conscience demands, and has a right to". Another criticism on this part of Dr Moberly's position is that he has inverted the true

sequence of effects. Punishment is not really first restorative, and then, if it fails, retributive, but first retributive, and then (may we hope) continued till it become restorative, so that in the end all evil shall disappear. That is the better version of Eternal Hope.

2. The vicarious penitence of the sinless Christ. Surely this conception is full of difficulty. No less than the doctrine of vicarious punishment, it involves the idea of the sin of the world being laid on Christ (as in Is. liii), and so far regards Him as representing mankind. The vicarious penitence of Christ, i.e. His penitence on our behalf, avails for the acceptance by God of the imperfect penitence of man. Here is a theory quite as distinctly substitutionary as that of vicarious endurance of punishment, involving the very difficulty which it professes to relieve. Its only recommendation is that it escapes the idea of penalty. Dr Moberly's beautiful but laboured illustration of the effect on an erring child of a sinless parent's penitence on the child's behalf is not to the point, so far at least as establishing the objective value towards God of the penitence of Christ for us. For, in the case of the parent, the penitence is of value purely for its subjective effect, its influence on the child.

3. If the Atonement consist in vicarious penitence, what is the need of the Cross, where is its connexion with penitence? There is much to be said on the influence of the Cross in awakening human penitence, but how are pain and death essential to the perfect penitence of the sinless Christ?

4. Dr Moberly completes his theory by reference

to the work of the Holy Spirit. The perfect penitence of the sinless Christ is communicated to the sinner by the Holy Spirit, and thus becomes the sinner's penitence. It is, of course, true that conviction of sin and penitence for sin are the work of the Spirit, but does this work of the Spirit necessarily presuppose the vicarious penitence of Christ? Certainly it is a new and unsupported suggestion that it should necessarily presuppose it.

Finally, I would say that, while there is much in the book which may help us to realise the effect of the Atonement on ourselves, it leaves the mystery of the Godward Atonement untouched, and does not solve the difficulties which attach to that, as to other Divine mysteries, which we in our present state are only capable of grasping so far as is practically necessary for our present life.

Let us, then, turn to the subjective aspect of the Cross, and more especially as it bears upon reconciliation, our reconciliation, the removal of our ignorance of God, and the misunderstanding and alienation from Him which arise from ignorance. In this reconciliation Christ is Mediator. Let us not pass over that word, so definitely and expressly put forward by St Paul. "There is one Mediator between God and man, Himself man, Christ Jesus" (I. Tim. ii. 5). In Canon Wilson's work quoted above we are bid to observe that there is no mediator in the parable of the Prodigal Son, and that therefore none is required. But much of what is so well said in the same passage as to Christ's work must be set against that incautious statement.

THE ATONEMENT

I should like here to protest strongly against the use of that parable to discredit the need of mediation. The interpretation of all parables must be guided by the understanding that the illustration given can never coincide precisely with the fact illustrated, but must either present some superfluity or some deficiency.

Christ is our Mediator. He has reconciled us to God by revealing to us the love of God. There are many who feel deeply the difficulty of believing in the love of God by reason of the difficulty which arises from contemplation of the evil and misery which are in the world. And there are still more in whom the sorrows and sufferings of their own lives shake that fundamental conviction. That God Himself in His Son should have taken human flesh in order to suffer and to die goes far to answer their doubts as to the love of God for man. There is not one of us, I am convinced, who realises fully what that answer means, and how complete it is. We describe reasoning to meet such difficulties by the name of Theodicy, or justification of the ways of God. The Cross is the great Theodicy. If God could will to do this, to endure this, we can believe in the perfectness of His love and wait for the explanation of the problem it presents to us. And here I must notice what Unitarians lose by the timidity of their faith. The value of the Cross as a Theodicy is gone if Jesus Christ was not truly God incarnate.

The Cross is a revelation of the love not only of God in His unity, but especially of Jesus Christ, the Son of God. The appeal which the Cross makes to our affections crowns and completes the appeal which is also made by the ministry and teaching of the Lord Jesus. Like the Evangelist, we behold His glory, full of grace and truth, manifest in His earthly life. And, with more insight than those who stood by, we behold a greater glory in His death. The very form of His Passion was fore-ordained that the visual image might be presented to all believers. He was lifted up that He might draw all men unto Him. And He was lifted up with arms outstretched. A familiar Latin hymn interprets His attitude thus: "Expandis orbi brachia". The translation in *Hymns A. & M.* is inadequate. His arms are outstretched to the world (*orbi*), not merely to His own people, to those who already believe. He draws men to Himself that they may know Him as the Way, the Truth, and the Life. Thus the Cross draws out from devout souls that personal love of the Lord Jesus Christ which has been not only an emotion, but a force manifested in a thousand forms of service, suffering, and victory. And what moves us so profoundly is not merely the anguish of Jesus our Lord and Master, but beyond and beneath it the meaning of it all: He suffers for us.

Again, there is the light which the sufferings and death of Christ throw upon human suffering in general. A Saviour who did not suffer, who did not die, could never have been taken to the heart of suffering humanity for its comfort and support. Even heathen religions, and Mahomedanism as well, show some consciousness of this, and have their martyrs. All human suffering is glorified for the believer as a partaking of the sufferings of Christ, and therefore the way to partaking of His glory. But, in regard to this aspect of Christ's death, we require a purpose implicit in it. Suffering is not of value in itself, far otherwise; it is of value as a means to an end. So, for the full subjective effect of the Cross, we need to be able to point to an objective work accomplished by it.

Lastly, on behalf of the objective character of the Atonement, I would appeal to Christian experience. Is that experience a delusion which testifies that in all ages the sinner overwhelmed with the consciousness of sin turns to the Cross? And the testimony is no less strong from the humble and faithful servants of God, whose deeper knowledge of their own hearts and of God's holiness makes the pardon and the love of God incredible to them apart from the one offering which takes away their sin. Is not the conviction of an ob-jective atonement embedded in all our greatest hymns, and does it not lie at the very foundation of the Sacrament of Holy Communion, and find expression in all Liturgies? At the same time we do not presume to say that any are excluded from the virtue of the Atonement who, while failing to accept the full doctrine of Scripture and the Church, nevertheless draw near to God as truly penitent children to their Father. The transcendent divine redemption embraces all penitents, apart from their consciousness of its full meaning. In the same way we may suppose that the virtue of the Cross extends to all communion between God and man both before and after the coming of Christ. For the Scripture tells us that in the timeless purpose of

God the Lamb was slain from the foundation of the world (Rev. xiii. 8, compared with Eph. i. 4 and I. Pet. i. 20). So Dante, following Aquinas, puts in brief the history of our salvation. God might simply by His clemency have put away our sin, but He chose to restore man to his perfect life by both His ways, by mercy and by justice, mercy in the Incarnation and justice in the Cross.[1]

The Cross has been from the first, and will continue to be, an "offence", to the Jews a stone of stumbling, and to the Greeks foolishness (I. Cor. i. 23). Proclaimed in its full significance, it is an offence still. Devout and learned men may labour in divers ways to remove the offence and, as they think, to make all things plain. But the full meaning and effect of the Cross go deeper than they suppose. It is not a stone on the surface, but a rock. Enough is revealed for faith to apprehend. The simpler and humbler our faith is, the nearer we shall come to the heart of the mystery, Christ crucified for us, the power of God, and the wisdom of God.

[1] *Paradiso*, vii. 103–120.

For EU product safety concerns, contact us at Calle de José Abascal, 56–1°,
28003 Madrid, Spain or eugpsr@cambridge.org.

www.ingramcontent.com/pod-product-compliance
Ingram Content Group UK Ltd.
Pitfield, Milton Keynes, MK11 3LW, UK
UKHW012328130625
459647UK00009B/137